Welcome to Your Married For A Purpose Reboot Facilitator's Guide™

Copyright © 2020 by Greg and Julie Gorman

All Scripture quotations are taken from the HOLY BIBLE, NEW INTERNATIONAL VERSION. Copyright © 1972, 1978, 1984 by Biblica. Used by permission of Biblica.

Published by Married For A Purpose, Hobe Sound, Florida.

Printed in the United States of America. All rights reserved under International Copyright Law. No part of this publication may be reproduced, stored in a retrieval system, or transmitted in any form or by any means-including electronic, photocopy, recording-without the prior written permission of the Married for a Purpose™. Thank you for your cooperation. Funding from this material assists Married for a Purpose to transform how culture views and values marriage and family.

Table of Contents

- A Note from Greg and Julie 1
- Before Your Meet Instructions 3
- Sample Reboot Weekend Letter for Couple 5
- Intake Questions for Couple 7
- Sample of Favorite's List for Couple 8
- Set the BIG Idea 9
- The Problem-Focused vs. Purpose-Focused Assessment 11

Day One
- What You Need to Facilitate 15
- Welcome Chart 16
- Set the Intention 18
- Best Practice & Hacks 21
- Where We Are 22
- Where We Want to Be 24
- What Got Us To Where We Are 27
- His/Hers/Our Interests 33
- Fun & Connection 36
- Core Values 39
- Marriage Mottos 43
- Learning and Checkpoints 47

Day Two
- Discover Him & Her 50
- Our Marriage Purpose 56
- Our Marriage Vision 60
- Manage for What's Best 65
- STOP Doing 69
- What's Next CHART 71
- Diffuse the Bombs in Your Marriage 77
- 3 Ways to Stay Connected. 78
- Parenting Principles for Every Season. 79
- When to Say Yes & No. 81
- Conversation Starters 82
- Final Check List 93
- Notes and End Notes 94

A Note from Greg and Julie

Hello Certified Coach!

We are so excited that you are uniting with us to restore the family, to instill hope, healing, and values where EVERY family member understands their worth, knows their value, and honors one another's design.

Get ready for a fun, at times challenging, yet incredible journey!

Working with couples isn't easy, but when you are called, and you step up and step out … GOD WILL SHOW UP! Our vision is to empower you in yours.

Your Married for A Purpose Marriage Reboot Retreat Certification provides a systematic and replicate-able process for you to lead husbands and wives towards greater unity and their shared desired outcome. Your certification manual outlines a wholistic process to help couples identify their purpose as a couple and learn how to build on common ground and fight for unity above all else.

As we begin, here are a few things we'd like to remind you of as you lead your couple through their personalized MARRIAGE REBOOT RETREAT.

1. **First and foremost, expect Favor.** God desires to help you. Lean into His wisdom. Seek His presence. Then, continue to welcome Him throughout the facilitation of each marriage reboot retreat.
2. **Remember, don't get sucked into the drama.** When you lead your Couple towards their desired outcome and don't get sucked into the drama of their differences and obstacles, you will welcome GOD'S BEST for EVERY Couple.
3. **Remember … trust the Process**. Ask questions that will lead your Couple towards their shared desired outcome. Help them build on common ground. Along the way, you

will need to tackle the proverbial elephant in the room, but behind every 'elephant,' GOD holds a promise.

4. **Be encouraged. Most couples agree on more than they disagree about … you just need to remind them.** Words like I imagine you both want … and then fill in the blank with *what we call NO BRAINERS* (like peace, joy, a strong legacy). Your no brainer question should proved a response that anyone would agree with; these no brainer questions will help keep your couple on track and moving forward in unity. Don't worry. We'll share best practices that we've learned over two decades of working with couples to help you facilitate each chart.

5. **In this book, in the top right corner of each chart, you will find expected timelines for each construct… however, remember EVERY chart is different for EVERY Couple.** Sometimes a couple takes a little longer on one chart but speeds through the next. So, lean in and manage the energy of what your couple needs, NOT the clock. Your overall MARRIAGE REBOOT RETREAT timeline eventually evens out.

6. **Before each chart, you'll notice suggestions to help you drive home a point or provide a value or truth for your couple, along with the central objective and desired outcome.** You should recognize the concept from your training but never hesitate to ask about it on our follow-up calls together.

7. **Finally, read the script for each chart colored in blue if you get stuck.**

Ok! Let's get started. Here are a few things you'll need to provide to your Couple before their MARRIAGE REBOOT RETREAT.

BEFORE YOU MEET & OTHER WAYPOINTS

As a facilitator, here are some of the WAYPOINTS you need to provide:

- ☐ INTAKE FORM of Questions Every Couple Should Ask

- ☐ A List of Favorites

- ☐ Information Letter for MARRIAGE REBOOT RETREAT with Your Tentative Schedule of Time Together

- ☐ Provide your Couple with the intake form, a list of favorites, and information regarding their MARRIAGE REBOOT RETREAT least a couple of weeks before meeting with them (unless you schedule a last-minute marriage reboot retreat).

- ☐ Also, don't forget to register your Couple to receive their packet for the MARRIAGE REBOOT RETREAT. You will need to provide MFAP with the Fee payment, along with the husband's name and email, the wife's name and email, your mailing address, and the date of the MARRIAGE REBOOT RETREAT to receive the Couple's package. Every package includes items you will need to facilitate their retreat and encouragement for them after the retreat, as follows:

    - o Two Participant Guides for Your Couple's MARRIAGE REBOOT RETREAT
    - o Access to their YEAR-LONG MFAP MEMBERSHIP.
    - o A Signed Copy of one of our marriage books.
    - o A Logoed MARRIAGE REBOOT RETREAT Portfolio for their Charts.

- ☐ While your Couple is with you, hand them the autographed book as a gift.
- ☐ Before your couple leaves verify that they can log in to access their videos in the membership at www.marriedforapurpose.com.
- ☐ Upon completing the MARRIAGE REBOOT RETREAT, please take photos of each chart and send them to gregandjulie@marriedforapurpose.com.
- ☐ Finally, upon Submitting their completed MARRIAGE REBOOT RETREAT (within seven to ten business days), you will receive a PDF of their

CUSTOMIZED MARRIAGE REBOOT RETREAT. When you receive the PDF, insert their personalized charts into the portfolio book, and either hand deliver it or ship it to them.

The following resources will help you craft a letter for your time with your couple. Modify as needed for each couple's MARRIAGE REBOOT RETREAT.

MARRIAGE REBOOT RETREAT Information Letter

Hi **(Insert the name of Spouse 1)** and **(the name of Spouse 2).** We are so excited to take this journey with you. No doubt you feel a bit anxious and yet excited about your MARRIAGE REBOOT RETREAT. Allow us to share more details of what to expect during our time together

Plan to arrive by 7 pm the night before our first day. On **(first day),** we will meet bright and early at 8:00 am for breakfast, share a time of devotion, and then get started. Here's an overview for …

DAY ONE:

- Set the intent for our time together.
- We'll unpack the three overarching principles for your marriage.
- Provide an assessment to reveal where your thoughts tend to gravitate.
- Identify WHAT YOU REALLY WANT for:
    - Your Marriage,
    - Career and Calling,
    - Faith,
    - Relationship with Family & Others,
    - Finances,
    - Communication,
    - Intimacy and
    - Your Overall Lifestyle / Life Rhythm.
- We'll dive deep to gain awareness of where you are, where you want to be, and what got you to where you are in your relationship.
- We'll also provide you with helpful ways to bridge the gaps in your relationship and build on Common Ground.
- You'll be surprised at your ability to create Shared Values and Marriage Mottos.

Every MARRIAGE REBOOT RETREAT is different, but we typically finish the day with a shared meal. You'll have a few things to reflect on and possible 'homework.' So, in preparation for day two, it'll be an early night. We will retreat and part ways by 7:30 pm to provide you time

for reflection, conversation, and time to unwind. We begin day two with breakfast, and a quick devotional at 8 am and then dive into the following …

DAY TWO:

- We'll explore the power of Your Combined Purpose and help you Define It.
- Unpack the Power of Vision and lead you to Create Your Combined Vision.
- Together, you'll Discover the POWER you each hold to Ensure Your Desired Outcome.
- We'll also provide tools to help you PROTECT Your Purpose.
- Identify Steps to PRIORITIZE Your Purpose.
- And list what you need to manage for and safeguard against, to live your Purpose.
- Before Day two concludes, you will gain a firm knowledge of your non-negotiables, and
- Together, develop a customized plan to live your discoveries to build a hope-filled legacy!

WHEW! We know it sounds like a lot … and … it is! BUT … it is A POWERFUL and PROVEN process that works. Know this; God is inviting you into partnership with HIM for YOUR PURPOSE. So, be ready to lean in and experience breakthroughs!

On a practical note:

- Dress comfortably.
- Bring a journal and pen.
- Bring a calendar for future assignments and scheduling.
- Be ready to be unplugged. NO electronics, cell phones, etc.

We are committed to praying, leading, and serving you with EVERYTHING we have, to help you EXPERIENCE a MARRIAGE REBOOT that you'll carry into EVERY area of life.

Let us know if you have any questions and thank you for entrusting us with your journey. We look forward to our time together and partnering with the Holy Spirit to help you step into ALL GOD has for your life and marriage.

The following intake form should be sent two weeks prior to meeting and received (ideally) no later than one week prior to your couple's reboot retreat.

What are you thankful for? What are the 3 greatest things happening in your life and marriage?
What are your pain points? Where do you feel you've failed; or feel a sense of guilt? Where do you feel stuck or misunderstood? What do you feel YOU need to change?
What do you HOPE for? What do you want more of in your life and marriage? If you could experience one thing right now, what do you want most for you and your spouse?
What could sabotage you from experiencing that change, and what one step do you feel you could take that would help you experience that change?
What would you like to happen through our time together? What is your ideal outcome or objective for our time together?
Are there any medical or clinical diagnoses we should be aware of as we enter this journey together?

Please return your questionnaire via email to **(INSERT YOUR EMAIL HERE)** one week prior to meeting with us but no less than 48 hours before your prescheduled session.

Your & Your Spouse's Name		
Your & Your Spouse's Cell phone		
Your & Your Spouse's Email		
Your & Your Spouse's Birthday		
What is your favorite cuisine(s)?		
What are your favorite Salty Snacks?		
What are your favorite Sweet Treats / Snacks?		
What is your favorite Candy?		
What is your favorite Dessert?		
What is your favorite Beverage?		
What is your favorite candle fragrance?		
What is your favorite restaurant?		
What's your favorite Relaxation Method?		
Are you on a special diet or any foods you are allergic to or dislike?		

Please return your questionnaire via email to **(INSERT YOUR EMAIL HERE)** one week prior to your reboot retreat.

Facilitator Note: A Week Before the MARRIAGE REBOOT RETREAT, send your client the Purpose focused Quiz so that they have it for a quick connect before the retreat. Schedule a 1-hour phone call to discuss details and the Purpose-Focused Quiz. This call will help you…

SET THE BIG IDEA AND PREPARATION

Prepare your client for an optimal experience by covering the following information:

- ☐ Share God's Intent For Their Marriage With THREE OVERARCHING PRINCIPLES (See The Following Script on page 10. But Feel Free To Paraphrase.

- ☐ Have Them Take The Quiz And Read The Results Of Their Purpose-Focused Assessment. (See Quiz In The Following Pages And The Explanation Of Their Results.)

- ☐ Remind Them Of To Dress Comfortable And What They Need To Bring.

- ☐ Review Timelines And Travel Details.

- ☐ Finally, Clarify Their Answers To The Favorites Questionnaire And Anything They Are Not Eating/Allergies.

See the following pages for the information you will need for this call.

Three Overarching Principles: What's the Big Idea?

God's Intent and A Few Reminders

God designed a purpose for your marriage.

- **God's Purpose includes …** A plan for <u>you</u>. A plan for <u>your spouse</u>. A plan for you as a <u>couple</u>.

- **Your Marriage Purpose:** Requires physical, emotional, and spiritual <u>interdependency</u> upon one another. It is *not something you need to do*; *it's a* <u>celebration</u> *of who you are* as a couple.

- **EVERY Couple exists to:**
    a. Make God <u>Known.</u>
    b. Bring God <u>Pleasure.</u> And, to …
    c. Demonstrate God's <u>Unconditional Love.</u>

The Problem-Focused/Purpose-Focused Assessment.

Share with your clients …

Let's take time to take and review a quick assessment together. Please grab your printed copy of the Purpose-Focused Assessment I sent to you. As a quick reminder, remember; this tool **is an awareness tool**. It's NOT good. It's NOT bad. It's merely an assessment to discern where your natural thought patterns tend to gravitate. So, as you take the Assessment, answer honestly and individually. Your answers should reflect as it pertains specifically to your marriage relationship. You'll notice two columns with a list of fifteen statements on each side. Choose which statement is MOST accurate. They may BOTH apply, but circle the side that resonates the most, from each line, separated in two columns.

Facilitator Note:

(This Assessment should only take about **15-20 minutes** to both do and read through your Couple's results. The purpose of this Assessment is to lightheartedly gain a greater awareness of where your Couple's minds tend to gravitate and reveal some of the opportunities they face in their overall mindset.)

Allow your Couple about **7-10 minutes** to circle their answers. Once your Couple finishes, read their results from the Assessment below.

Problem-Focused / Purpose-Focused Assessment

1. I see my Spouse's shortcomings, flaws, and weaknesses.	1. I see differences in me and my Spouse that complement and balance one another.
2. My Spouse's idiosyncrasies constantly annoy me.	2. I extend grace because I need grace. I choose to believe the best about my Spouse, celebrating their design.
3. I tend to complain about the present and the past.	3. I intentionally practice praise, looking with positive expectancy toward the future. I'm not bound by un-forgiveness.
4. I feel hindered.	4. I focus on God's promises. They offer me strength and hope.
5. I lack clarity and am confused by current circumstances.	5. I am seeking clear direction and certainty of where I want to go.
6. I tend to see glitches, hitches, and difficulties.	6. I practice an attitude of gratitude and praise.
7. I contemplate and point out the ways my Spouse should change.	7. I ask God to help my Spouse live fully into His design for their life. I choose to focus on improving, knowing I can only change myself.
8. I feel trapped.	8. I see options and seek God to make positive changes in my life.
9. I justify my actions by pointing to My Spouse's faults.	9. I refuse to keep a scoreboard and take accountability to change and grow ME.
10. I regret marrying my Spouse.	10. God designed a purpose for my marriage and uses my marriage to make me stronger.
11. Our past and present circumstances hinder us from serving others.	11. The entirety of our life serves a purpose.
12. We spend the majority of our time trying to fix one another.	12. We practice healthy self-examination and genuinely seek to grow together.
13. I feel burdened to make things happen.	13. I'm faithful where God positions me.
14. I often pray; surely, there must be more to life than this.	14. I most often pray; Father open the doors You want me to walk through.
15. I tend to compare and compete, feeling unworthy or inadequate.	15. I embrace our unique designs and love using our talents for God's glory.

Now that you've circled your answers. Take a moment to write "Problem" on the top line before the word "Focused" on the left-hand side of the page. Then, write "Purpose" on the top line before the word "Focused: on the right-hand side of the page. Now, tally the number of times you highlighted a statement from the Right-handed Column. Talley your scores and share the number of times you circled a statement from the right-hand side. **Spouse One**, how many did you circle from the right-hand Column? **Spouse Two**, how about you? Read the paragraph that correlates with each of their specific results based on the number they tallied from the right-hand Column.

- If you scored 13-15, congrats! You firmly believe God destined you for greatness and aren't intimidated to live it! You master your thoughts. More than likely, people single you out as an optimist. You probably hold a keen idea of God's Purpose for your life and love your marriage. Keep up the good work and maintain your humility. You're well on your way to discovering God's exact Purpose for your marriage if you haven't already.

- If you scored 10-12, bravo! You generally believe God designed you for a distinct purpose. You tend to focus on what is good over the bad and aren't afraid to practice discipline to ensure you control your thoughts. You enjoy your Spouse and share great expectancy towards your future. You genuinely desire significance yet, at times, find yourself lost in the specifics. No worries. Continue to take every thought captive to the cross, and in due time, you will reap great rewards. Keep on keeping on—your distinct marriage purpose awaits you.

- If you scored 7-9, you're a fighter, determined to press forward. You often find yourself frustrated, wanting to be further along and freer in your thoughts, but don't get discouraged. Use your energy to meet with God in prayer. Invite Him to continue to change the things needing to be changed. When you can't change the way you feel, you need to change the way you think. Practice believing the best about your Spouse. Speak the power of God's Word over your relationship. Choose to accept that God designed a purpose for your marriage, and you will find it. We are so excited for you to experience greater breakthroughs throughout the remainder of this book.

- If you scored 6 or below, recognize your natural tendency focuses on the problems that seem to bombard you in your everyday thinking. You try to be positive but feel powerless to the problems surrounding your life. At times you may feel forgotten, defeated, and short-changed. You may readily recognize obstacles or barriers out of your control that keep you from moving forward in the direction you want to move. Remember, God has not given you a spirit of timidity but the power of a strong mind. Submit your thoughts to Him in prayer. Take time every day to meditate on the truth that God created you and your Spouse on Purpose for a purpose. Claim the promises of His word and never give up. God uses all things for the good of those who love Him.[i] He fights for you and will help you protect what the enemy tries to steal. You truly are destined for greatness. God designed a purpose for you and your Spouse, and we can't wait for Him to reveal it to you.

Facilitator Note: As you close the call, remind them that the Assessment they just took is merely an AWARENESS tool. It is not good or bad. It just is! It's where they are and helps you as a facilitator to identify where their mind tends to gravitate. Let them know how excited you are to see them. And ask if they have any final questions. ☺

DAY ONE

What You Will Need to Facilitate:

- ☐ Sharpie Markers https://amzn.to/3rFIIwo
- ☐ Painter's Tape to Hang Charts https://amzn.to/3uTBua7
- ☐ White Correction Tape https://amzn.to/3Ln4MUb
- ☐ An Easel for Flip Chart https://amzn.to/3A2bbzW or https://amzn.to/3HExw8t

On the day of (or the day before), be sure to do the following:

SET THE ENVIRONMENT:

- ☐ Display their Drawn Charts before they arrive
- ☐ Tissues
- ☐ Beverages
- ☐ Snacks
- ☐ Shop for-and Fill the Room with their favorite Snacks and Scents

As you create your charts, match the following colors with each domain to provide consistency in your charting.

- ➢ **MARRIAGE: DARK BLUE**
- ➢ **CAREER / CALLING: RED**
- ➢ **FAITH: PURPLE**
- ➢ **FAMILY & EXTENDED RELATIONSHIPS: ORANGE**
- ➢ **FINANCIAL: LIGHT GREEN**
- ➢ **COMMUNICATION: BLACK**
- ➢ **INTIMACY / SEX: LIGHT BLUE**
- ➢ **LIFESTYLE RHYTHM (Health/Recreation/Life Rhythm): DARK GREEN**

Before meeting your Couple on Day One, take time to pray. Seek a CENTRAL SCRIPTURE to GUIDE YOUR COUPLES MARRIAGE REBOOT RETREAT. Your first chart sets the tone for your Couple's MARRIAGE REBOOT RETREAT.

The Purpose of your WELCOME CHART is to:

- ☐ Communicate you preparation to receive them and to set the tone of what you believe GOD desires for this Couple to meditate on throughout your time together.
- ☐ Invite God to share a verse that will assist your Couple to receive and grow and welcome GOD'S BEST during your time together and following the retreat.

A Great Best Practice:

- ☐ Pray and reflect for 2-3 days before the MARRIAGE REBOOT RETREAT preparation of leading each Couple as a couple. Ask, God, what do you want to share with them? What do they need to know? How do they need encouraged?
- ☐ As you prepare to receive the Couple, ask GOD's wisdom to provide a Scripture that offers wisdom, encouragement, or a hard charge to action.
- ☐ When a passage, thought, or concept comes to mind, research it. Sometimes we've had an idea like, *Encourage your Couple, they can trust Me.* Other times we've had specific SCRIPTURES come to mind, like *Be strong and courageous.* Follow the Holy Spirit's prompting and find a verse that matches what He reveals.
- ☐ Then create their welcome chart.

WELCOME

To create your Couple's *WELCOME CHART,* be sure to:

- ➢ HIGHLIGHT YOUR COUPLE'S NAMES,
- ➢ DATE of the MARRIAGE REBOOT RETREAT,
- ➢ YOUR NAME,
- ➢ AND THEIR MARRIAGE REBOOT RETREAT BIBLE VERSE
- ➢ **Write NEAT and LEGIBLY.** Your presentation matters and is essential to help our administrative team accurately capture each chart.
- ➢ Remember, colors evoke emotions and help create a rhythm for your Couple. Use the suggested color schemes that we provide throughout your MARRIAGE REBOOT RETREAT TRAINING MANUAL.

The first page of your chart should look like the following. (Replace the specifics of your Couple in the appropriate spaces.)

Husband's name & Wife's name

Marriage Reboot Retreat

Facilitated by: Your Name & Your Spouse's Name

Reboot VERSE

The MONTH and DAY (of the reboot), along with the YEAR

(Example)

Johnathon & Sarah Maxwell

Marriage Reboot Retreat

Facilitated by: Greg & Julie Gorman

Proverbs 3:5-6

January 27, 2021

SET THE INTENTION

When you meet on the morning of the first day, set the intention of your time together. **The Purpose of "Setting the Intention"** is to make sure your Couple feels safe, accepted, and ready to dive into pursuing GOD'S best. Couples are looking to answer three questions:

- Am I safe, and can I trust you and will you judge me?
- Can you really help me, and do you really understand where I am and what I am feeling?
- Is what I want possible?

They may be thinking, *Boy, I sure hope my Spouse is listening,* or *I sure hope these guys let them know how much he or she is messing up and fixes them.*

So, you want to make sure you set the intent. See the script below to understand better how to explain the Married for a Purpose Philosophy and why this retreat is different than any other they've probably experienced. The script is for you, but feel free to capture its essence and make it your own.

Here is a Script to Briefly Describe the Married for A Purpose Philosophy:

As we share time, a few distinctions make this MARRIAGE REBOOT RETREAT different from other marriage encounters. Though we'll take time to gain awareness of your life learnings and what created your belief system, most of our time will concentrate on your desired outcome instead of your problems.

After all, all thought leaders agree that we become what we think about and find what we are looking for, or as we like to say, we gravitate towards what we contemplate. So, we want to spend most of our time together concentrating on what we really want, not on what we don't want. Don't get us wrong; problems will be addressed but in a unique way. You see, we look at problems to identify and understand *what we **don't** want.* They provide us with awareness to look for and find *what we **do** want*, together, with God. So, we'll lead you to discover the things you agree about. We'll frequently ask questions and discern what you both agree you desire

as a couple. We'll look for what you want and every opportunity to build on common ground. We'll share ideas like, you gravitate towards what you contemplate ... which begs your decision to focus on what is true, lovely, and of a good report. We want to help you do that and help teach you **how to think** ... not **what to think.** When you take captive every thought and unite towards what you both want and God's desire ... BREAKTHROUGH HAPPEN! So ...
Here are a few GROUND RULES to optimize our outcome together:

- During our time together, we want to encourage you to ... See the Best. Believe the Best. And Speak the Best. Time Magazine wrote an article to highlight what couples long for in a spouse. Every Spouse desires a spouse who sees them for who they are, accepts them for who they are while bringing out the best in who they are.

- Find what you love, not what's lacking.

- Be accountable for yourself.

- We will frequently remind you to build on common ground and continually reflect on questions like:
    1. What is our desired outcome? What do you both want?
    2. What compromise can you make to honor one another and build your relationship?
    3. What's each of your parts to welcome your desired outcome?

- This Process includes a Wholistic approach to life and marriage. We will identify what you both want in the following areas: Marriage / Career / Faith / Your Relationship with Family and Others and additional areas like finances, communication, intimacy, and your overall lifestyle rhythm.

- We want to encourage you to utilize page 30, entitled REBOOT LEARNINGS. During our time together, you will discover truths or learnings you ALWAYS want to remember or NEVER want to forget. Be sure to document any of your *AHA moments or thoughts that make you think; WOW ... THAT was GOOD! I NEVER want to forget that! OR I ALWAYS want to remember that!*

- You'll also want to create a list of CHECKPOINTS that will help you change your current habits from what you don't want to what you do want. For example: When we run into conflict or need to talk about something, we often say; *I may not say this perfectly … or … Are you at a place for us to talk about something I need help with …?* Or on days we woke up on the wrong side of the bed and feel a little grumpy, rather than taking it out on one another, we've learned to say preventatively; *Hey, I need to give you a heads up, I'm feeling off a little today …*

- In other words, CHECKPOINTS are like LEARNINGS but help you answer … what can I do when this happens? Or what is a small pivot I can make to cause a better outcome? It may be something as simple as … when I feel angry, I will pause and ask myself; do I want to fight, or do I want to unite? It may be that you need to affirm your Spouse by using words like; I am listening. I hear you! Or ask; How can I help?

- Aside from page 29, also look at your AT A GLANCE PAGE located on page 8. This single chart is designed to capture strategic takeaways like your Scripture, Core Values, Purpose, Vision, and Life Mottos. It is a great page to review upon the conclusion of your MARRIAGE REBOOT RETREAT and will be provided in your personalized portfolio. The At a Glance Chart will serve as a helpful tool to stay on track and build on common ground.

Facilitator Note:

As you, the facilitator, begin with the end in mind. Remember, as you facilitate each chart, observe and listen for passions, purpose, and get a feel for who they are and who God designed them to be, together. Tomorrow as you approach "purpose" you'll leverage your overall observations to offer insight and direction as they craft their 12 word or less purpose based on the evidence and your observation.

*Facilitator Note: Best Practices / Hacks

As you journey forward, leading your couple towards their combined desired outcome, there may be times along the way they feel in opposition and operate like opponents vs. partners. If so, here are some best practices.

- Don't try to FIX your clients. Create a path to healing and wholeness.
- Trust the Process. If you get stuck, remember your job is to facilitate and ask questions.
- Don't let them suck you into their DRAMA. Instead, point them towards common ground and desired outcomes.
- When at all possible, validate both spouses that they are justified in *how* they feel *what* they feel. Then, point them towards hope and healing by building on common ground.
- Use the process to hold the conversations needing to be held.
- Ask NO brainer questions to illustrate how much your couple shares in common. You might say something like; sometimes, when we work with couples, they declare that they SHARE NOTHING in common until we begin to ask questions like: do you both want more fun? Connection? Greater intimacy? Do you both want to feel respected? Do you both want to feel Loved? Do you want to laugh more, play more, and break up the monotony of life? Unanimously they all begin to identify how they share a lot in common.
- Take time to encourage your couples to Celebrate … Don't Just Tolerate One Another's Differences.
- Ask them point-blank:
  (HUSBAND) do you want to make your wife feel loved, respected, and cherished? Do you desperately want her to know how much you care and appreciate all she does? Do you sometimes forget to express your love and admiration? Do you sometimes get stuck in knowing how to express your respect?
  (WIFE) do you want to make your husband feel loved and respected? Do you desperately want him to know how much you care and admire him? Do you sometimes get stuck in knowing how to express your respect?
- If your Couple needs a little encouragement and more time in this area, you may help them by asking them to highlight their strengths and their Spouse's strengths by asking; what are your strengths? What are your Spouse's strengths? How can you leverage one another's Strengths?
- If your Couple is disconnected, point out what you've observed and how they can work well together. OR … Share how you and your Spouse vary in design and how you've learned to maximize those differences.
- Use the illustration of how when iron sharpens iron, there is friction, but the friction causes the blade to be sharp and powerful. Or how the diversity of the team is its strength.

Each *hack* or *best practice* will help to serve you as you, lead your Couple to celebrate their design & build toward their combined desired outcome together!

Ok. Time for your FIRST OFFICIAL CHART that you'll FACILITATE.

(WHERE WE ARE CHART- Expected Timeline: 30 Minutes - 1 Hour)

The Purpose Of The *WHERE WE ARE CHART* Is To: Revisit the strategic questions your Couple answered and submitted before their MARRIAGE REBOOT RETREAT.

Facilitator Note: Prior to your Couple arriving, chart their responses. Combine what they both shared from their submissions. Read what you combined from their submissions and ask if anything is missing from each section (thankful for/ pain points/ and hope for). **It's NOT unusual for pain points to surface. Slow down.** Unpack what you need to gain perspective. Ask the Couple to expand on any area you need greater clarity around. When you need more information, a great statement to make is: Tell me more about that. Notice some of the reminders of doing what we can, and that if we want something different, we need to do something different. ☺

WHERE WE ARE CHART
(Page 9 of your couple's reboot workbook)

What are you thankful for?	
Your PAIN Points: We rarely change until the pain of staying the same exceeds the pain of change … AND … If we want something different, we need to do something different. Don't let what you can't do, stop you from remembering what you CAN DO …	
What WE BOTH HOPE FOR & WANT:	

Example:

WHERE WE ARE

What are you thankful for?	Family We both are still trying Faith Health Fun vacation with our kids recently
Your PAIN Points: We rarely change until the pain of staying the same exceeds the pain of change … AND … If we want something different, we need to do something different. Don't let what you can't do, stop you from remembering what you CAN DO …	We constantly misunderstand one another Haven't had sex for months Living two separate lives Nothing seems fun Need spontaneity Lack of communication and connection
What WE BOTH HOPE FOR & WANT:	Fun Connection One-ness Travel To feel like we love one another again Sexual Intimacy Unity in parenting A secure financial one-ness

(WHERE WE WANT TO BE- Expected Timeline: 1 ½ hours)

The Purpose Of The *WHERE WE WANT TO BE CHART* Is To: Solidify what your couple shares in common that they both want for every facet of their relationship.

Here is an opening SCRIPT to transition into your next chart:

We are about to spend the next 36-48 hours creating a plan for your life and marriage. Let's identify one thing you'd both like to put a plan to get us started. As we chart your SHARED DESIRED OUTCOMES, let's use sentences like, we'd like to:

- ☐ … devise a plan for …
- ☐ … create a system for …or
- ☐ … decide a strategy around…
- ☐ … define a process …
- ☐ … obtain clarity for … or
- ☐ … gain wisdom surrounding a decision we need to make … or
- ☐ … determine the direction we want to take …

We want to encourage you.

- ⇒ We will spend the next two days developing a plan for your marriage, so don't hold back.
- ⇒ Don't think of what's possible. Instead, in each area of your life, we want to capture in a single sentence what you REALLY desire … and are willing to fight for … as a couple.
- ⇒ Don't let '*what has been*' stop you from claiming what GOD desires.

So, in a single sentence, tell us what you want for your life and marriage … (Capture their response for each area listed on the WHERE WE WANT TO BE CHART.)

(WHERE WE WANT TO BE - Expected Timeline: 1 ½ hours)

WHERE WE WANT TO BE

(What Do We Both Want?)

MARKAGE	CAREER / CALLING
A plan for ...	A vision and greater clarity in ...

What's our desired outcome? What do we want to create a plan, process, strategy for, or gain wisdom or clarity around the following areas?

FAITH	FAMILY & EXTENDED RELATIONSHIPS
A strategy to ...	A process to ...

FINANCES	COMMUNICATION
A strategy to ...	A process for ...

What's our desired outcome? What do we want to create a plan, process, strategy for, or gain wisdom or clarity around the following areas?

INTIMACY/SEX	LIFESTYLE / RHYTHM (Health/Recreation/Fun)
A plan for ...	Gain clarity on how to ...

You can finish this chart by asking: Is there anything missing you'd like to add to the chart concerning your physical, intellectual, emotional, relational, or spiritual well-being?

Example:

WHERE WE WANT TO BE

(What Do We Both Want?)

MARRIAGE

A plan to unify our strengths and love one another well.

CAREER / CALLING

Gain clarity for defined roles.

What's our desired outcome? What do we want to create a plan, process, or strategy for ...or gain wisdom or clarity around in the following areas?

FAITH

Create a strategy to share our faith in our home.

FAMILY & EXTENDED RELATIONSHIPS

Identify people that we both would like to build friendship with together.

FINANCES

A strategy to build a stable and secure financial future, together.

COMMUNICATION

Gain wisdom on how to communicate with respect and love toward one another.

What's our desired outcome? What do we want to create a plan, process, or strategy for ...or gain wisdom or clarity around in the following areas?

INTIMACY/SEX

A plan to connect with respect and spend quality time where we both feel special.

LIFESTYLE / Rhythm: (Recreation/Time/Fun)

Gain clarity on new ways to reconnect and enjoy a healthy rhythm for life, together.

Facilitator Note: Great JOB Facilitators. As we prepare for The **WHAT GOT US HERE CHART. The Purpose of the chart is to help you better understand the context of your Couple's journey together and to give your couple the opportunity to talk about what they want to talk about.** (You'll find the actual chart on page 31.) Before facilitating this chart, here are a few things to keep in mind to help produce an optimal outcome:

- ⇒ It will be critical for you to remain neutral and attentive to the hidden messages conveyed during the process. The objective, allow each Spouse to feel HEARD, VALIDATED, UNDERSTOOD. Nothings worse than being misunderstood. Many clients enter this Process feeling misunderstood. As a facilitator you want what's been *miscommunicated or not communicated* to be unpacked in such a way that both husband and wife feel listened to, understood, and validated and begin the Process where they start to do that for one another.

- ⇒ Document what happened and specific thoughts or feelings your couple shares. Listen for comments like, "I never." Or "I always." Or "I just can't understand why they would…" These comments will help you identify clues of what needs reinforced to bring about good results and help you address any toxic behaviors or beliefs hindering your Couple.

- ➢ No matter how outlandish the sin, story, or setback … do NOT judge. Use wisdom and kindness to demonstrate empathy, wisdom, and understanding.

- ➢ As their facilitator, always consider what they need to know, feel, and do, to experience breakthrough and create new habits for living.

- ➢ From your own life, leverage short thoughts that point them to scenarios that let them know you can understand, and what helped you.

- Ask their Spouse for their perspective and then build on common ground and help them land on WISDOM and NEW truths.

- Practice great restraint. Don't get sucked into the drama. Instead, leverage the power of the Holy Spirit to highlight the truth of HIS perspective.

- If dissension arises, lead with what we call NO BRAINER QUESTIONS, like: You never intentionally meant to hurt your Spouse; did you? But I'm sure you can understand that when this happened why that disrupted the thing you meant to communicate like PEACE/JOY/RESPECT/ Unconditional love; right?

- During the leading forward, try to take the STING out of their *SPECIFICS,* by leveraging truths like; you ONLY want to communicate peace, right? You want to experience true joy and unity, right? Leverage thoughts like; you both want to have fun, right? You both desire greater connection, intimacy, and want to create an environment where you both feel loved and laugh more, right?

- As you move forward, play out scenarios that leverage respect for one another. Ask them what their part was in the disagreement. If they need help, respectfully provide suggestions, and watch for agreement.

Ok here is a script you can use to introduce the WHAT GOT US HERE CHART.

Share: As we start this next chart, we want to pause and reflect on what we've done so far. First, we gained awareness of where we you are. Then, we identified where you want to be. As we move into this next chart, we want to get to know you more and understand **HOW** and **WHY** you think, **WHAT** you think. The purpose of this chart is to hear more of your story and gain perspective of why you believe what you believe; examine it and discover the truth and grow. So, we're going to unpack what got you to this point and your belief system, for the Purpose of gaining awareness. As we do that, it's important to understand how beliefs are formed.

Beliefs are formed in three ways:

- **First, someone we love, or respect tells us something and we believe it.**
- **Second, Our Life Experience. We do something, and the results of what happened because we did that something forms a belief.**
- **The third way is by repetition. Someone (sometimes ourselves) repeats something over and over and we come to believe it.**

As we unpack this next chart, we want to remind you that there are some beliefs that have gotten you stuck. But here's great news … *though your past shapes you, it does not need to define you.* God holds your future and wants you UNSTUCK!

You've identified what your central desired outcome is, so we are going to leverage this next chart to identify the things that have tripped you up, that you need breakthrough, to get you from *where you are* to *where you want to be*, by better identifying *what got you here*.

So, here's your chance to share together; what keeps you from moving forward to where you want to be. Or what trips you up?

Facilitator Note: Reference your Couple's, WHERE WE ARE CHART and WHERE WE WANT TO BE CHART read a specific part from what needs changed or confused and say … Tell me about that.

Questions to Ask:

- What trips you up or hinders your unity as a couple?
- Where do you feel stuck that you just don't seem to be able to quite overcome?
- Where's the bottleneck from here to there?
- What causes you hesitation or resistance?

If it gets to heavy, change the energy, as needed. Here are some helpful questions:

- When have you felt the most loved by your Spouse?
- What qualities do you love most about your Spouse?
- When do you feel the most supported?
- What makes you feel empowered?
- What are your favorite memories, or timelines in your relationship and why; what was happening?

Facilitator Note: In the TAKEAWAY SECTION enter what they learned and what they want to remember as NEW truths for their relationship. Help them identify any themes that you've observed.

Share your thoughts and ask the following questions as needed:

- What would God want you to remember or change in your beliefs? What is the TRUTH that He would say about your circumstance or His desire for you as a couple?
- What other truths do you realize from today's perspective?
- How can you replace what tripped you up from the past with new truths, and new understanding gained during our time together?

The WHAT GOT US HERE CHART usually takes anywhere between 1 ½ to 2 hours)

WHAT GOT US HERE? (Page 16 in their workbook_

HIM	HER	New Truth To Remember

Example:

WHAT GOT US HERE?

HIM	HER	New Truth to Remember
No Sex Always chooses kids over me.	His harshness with me and the kids. Nothing is ever good enough.	We both want our kids to know they are loved and valued. We want one another to know we are loved and valued. We need to prioritize one another and our intimacy.
Loss job. She's distant. Never has sex.	His Infidelity. His Porn	We have harbored bitterness and resentment. We will seek GOD'S BEST in and out of the bedroom.
Planned Dates	Time with Kids	We will be intentional about quality time with one another and put boundaries in place. We will schedule other times with the kids to have intentional connection with them.
Boat trip Valentine's Day	Hutchinson' Island Vacation	We feel the most loved when we plan get away retreats.
This REBOOT RETREAT	This REBOOT RETREAT	We thrive when we seek to understand one another. We really do want the same things.

At the end of this chart, you may decide to provide an Extra **Homework** Assignment from one of the following, **if needed**:

- ☐ Write a note to one another of how you want to be seen and known as, to your children and your spouse.
- ☐ Write a note to one another of what you appreciate and value about your Spouse.

(This chart should take approximately 20-30 minutes)

The Purpose of the following charts reveal your couple's interests to help them connect. Instruct your couple to turn to pages 17-18 and check every box they enjoy individually in their book. When they are done, take a picture of each of their charts from their individual books so that they can be added to their portfolio book. Then combine their shared interests on the combined interest flip chart.

HIS INTERESTS

Spiritual	Acts of Service	Sports	Other Interests
☐ Administration	☐ Business Planning	☐ Softball/Baseball	☐ Gardening
☐ Mentoring/Discipleship	☐ Caring for infants	☐ Swimming	☐ Dancing
☐ Attending retreats/conferences	☐ Cooking	☐ Golf	☐ Reading
☐ Gifts of the Spirit	☐ Cleaning	☐ Tennis	☐ Drawing
☐ Community outreach	☐ Greeting	☐ Motor Cycling	☐ Traveling
☐ International outreach	☐ Arts & Media / Videography	☐ Working Out	☐ Being Outdoors
☐ Bible studies	☐ Photography	☐ Volleyball	☐ Fishing
☐ Prayer/Intercession	☐ Restoring Things	☐ Basketball	☐ Hunting/Shooting
☐ Teaching adults	☐ Decorating	☐ Biking	☐ Boating
☐ Teaching children	☐ Planning Events	☐ Running/Walking	☐ Playing an Instrument
☐ Preaching / public speaking	☐ Organizing	☐ Bowling	☐ Watching Movies
☐ Coaching	☐ Painting	☐ Aerobics	☐ Music/Art
☐ Evangelism/Witnessing	☐ Fixing broken things	☐ Yoga	☐ History
☐ Worshiping	☐ Building/Working w/ hands	☐ Canoe/Kayaking	☐ Shopping
☐ Writing	☐ Sewing, Knitting, Crochet	☐ Hiking	☐ Exploring
☐ Singing	☐ Plumbing	☐ Caving	☐ Graphic design
☐ Leading	☐ Roofing/Construction	☐ Surfing	☐ Camping
☐ Encouraging	☐ Feeding the hungry	☐ Snorkeling/Suba Diving	☐ RV'ing
☐ Hospitality	☐ Creating/Designing	☐ Pickle Ball	☐ Sex
☐ Listening to Podcasts	☐ Financial Planning	☐ Paddle Boarding	☐ Puzzles
☐ Giving Financially	☐ Printing	☐ Tow Water Sports	☐ Bird Watching
☐ Educating	☐ Computer	☐ Parasailing	☐ Visiting the Zoo
☐ Ideating / Masterminds	☐ Publishing/Editing	☐ Zip lining	☐ Bird Watching
☐ Government	☐ Entrepreneurship	☐ Snow Skiing	☐ Other
		☐ Snow Mobile	

HER INTERESTS

Spiritual	Acts of Service	Sports	Other Interests
☐ Administration	☐ Business Planning	☐ Softball/Baseball	☐ Gardening
☐ Mentoring/Discipleship	☐ Caring for infants	☐ Swimming	☐ Dancing
☐ Attending retreats/conferences	☐ Cooking	☐ Golf	☐ Reading
☐ Gifts of the Spirit	☐ Cleaning	☐ Tennis	☐ Drawing
☐ Community outreach	☐ Greeting	☐ Motor Cycling	☐ Traveling
☐ International outreach	☐ Arts & Media / Videography	☐ Working Out	☐ Being Outdoors
☐ Bible studies	☐ Photography	☐ Volleyball	☐ Fishing
☐ Prayer/Intercession	☐ Restoring Things	☐ Basketball	☐ Hunting/Shooting
☐ Teaching adults	☐ Decorating	☐ Biking	☐ Boating
☐ Teaching children	☐ Planning Events	☐ Running/Walking	☐ Playing an Instrument
☐ Preaching / public speaking	☐ Organizing	☐ Bowling	☐ Watching Movies
☐ Coaching	☐ Painting	☐ Aerobics	☐ Music/Art
☐ Evangelism/Witnessing	☐ Fixing broken things	☐ Yoga	☐ History
☐ Worshiping	☐ Building/Working w/ hands	☐ Canoe/Kayaking	☐ Shopping
☐ Writing	☐ Sewing, Knitting, Crochet	☐ Hiking	☐ Exploring
☐ Singing	☐ Plumbing	☐ Caving	☐ Graphic design
☐ Leading	☐ Roofing/Construction	☐ Surfing	☐ Camping
☐ Encouraging	☐ Feeding the hungry	☐ Snorkeling/Suba Diving	☐ RV'ing
☐ Hospitality	☐ Creating/Designing	☐ Pickle Ball	☐ Sex
☐ Listening to Podcasts	☐ Financial Planning	☐ Paddle Boarding	☐ Puzzles
☐ Giving Financially	☐ Printing	☐ Tow Water Sports	☐ Bird Watching
☐ Educating	☐ Computer	☐ Parasailing	☐ Visiting the Zoo
☐ Ideating / Masterminds	☐ Publishing/Editing	☐ Zip lining	☐ Bird Watching
☐ Government	☐ Entrepreneurship	☐ Snow Skiing	☐ Other
		☐ Snow Mobile	

(This chart should take approximately 20-30 minutes)

Facilitator Note: The Purpose of this chart is to help them create ideas of how to date one another, surprise one another and intentionally connect. Chart their combined interests and share the following Ideas for Building on them. Plan Surprise Dates. His Date Night. Her Date Night. Embrace Spontaneity. Planned Get-Away Dates. Choose different shared interests and ask them how they would like to plan for FUN & CONNECTION together.

OUR COMBINED INTERESTS

Spiritual	Acts of Service	Sports	Other Interests
☐ Administration	☐ Business Planning	☐ Softball/Baseball	☐ Gardening
☐ Mentoring/Discipleship	☐ Caring for infants	☐ Swimming	☐ Dancing
☐ Attending retreats/conferences	☐ Cooking	☐ Golf	☐ Reading
☐ Gifts of the Spirit	☐ Cleaning	☐ Tennis	☐ Drawing
☐ Community outreaches	☐ Greeting	☐ Motor Cycling	☐ Traveling
☐ International outreaches	☐ Arts & Media / Videography	☐ Working Out	☐ Being Outdoors
☐ Bible studies	☐ Photography	☐ Volleyball	☐ Fishing
☐ Prayer/Intercession	☐ Restoring Things	☐ Basketball	☐ Hunting/Shooting
☐ Teaching adults	☐ Decorating	☐ Biking	☐ Boating
☐ Teaching children	☐ Planning Events	☐ Running/Walking	☐ Playing an Instrument
☐ Preaching / public speaking	☐ Organizing	☐ Bowling	☐ Watching Movies
☐ Coaching	☐ Painting	☐ Aerobics	☐ Music/Art
☐ Evangelism/Witnessing	☐ Fixing broken things	☐ Yoga	☐ History
☐ Worshiping	☐ Building/Working w/ hands	☐ Canoe/Kayaking	☐ Shopping
☐ Writing	☐ Sewing, Knitting, Crochet	☐ Hiking	☐ Exploring
☐ Singing	☐ Plumbing	☐ Caving	☐ Graphic design
☐ Leading	☐ Roofing/Construction	☐ Surfing	☐ Camping
☐ Encouraging	☐ Feeding the hungry	☐ Snorkeling/Suba Diving	☐ RV'ing
☐ Hospitality	☐ Creating/Designing	☐ Pickle Ball	☐ Sex
☐ Listening to Podcasts	☐ Financial Planning	☐ Paddle Boarding	☐ Puzzles
☐ Giving Financially	☐ Printing	☐ Tow Water Sports	☐ Bird Watching
☐ Educating	☐ Computer	☐ Parasailing	☐ Visiting the Zoo
☐ Ideating / Masterminds	☐ Publishing/Editing	☐ Zip lining	☐ Bird Watching
☐ Government	☐ Entrepreneurship	☐ Snow Skiing	☐ Other
		☐ Snow Mobile	

FUN & CONNECTION CHART

Share:

The Purpose of this next chart is to help you identify and create a **FUN** lifestyle rhythm. In His book, replenish, Lance Witt highlights the importance of replenishment. The truth is **MOST** couples lack connection.

We crowd our life with busy activities but the more we crowd our life the more we crowd our room for connection. The busier we are the less likely we are to extend grace to one another. We busy ourselves and crowd our margin, and inadvertently lessen our ability to accept one another's imperfections.

As couples, if we truly want a thriving vibrant marriage, we need to stop crowding our life with a bunch of *GOT*-TO'S; simplify our schedules and make room for more GET-TOS.

'GOT TOS' makes you feel like; *here's one more thing we* **have** *to do!* 'GET-TOS' add margin, inspiration, and foster FUN and CONNECTION.

"GET TO'S" help to provide a **sustainable rhythm for your life and marriage**.

1. So, when you feel depleted, what refuels you and replenishes you to feel alive and enjoy life more? What inspires and refuels you?

2. What activity would add FUN?

3. What would help you connect and help you feel inspired, refueled, or at peace?

4. How can you intentionally add these activities to the rhythm of your life, together? Individually? With Others?

(This chart should take approximately 20-30 minutes. Use the chart to capture ideas for couples to have fun, connect, and replenish together.)

FUN & CONNECTION CHART!

Together
1.
2.
3.

Individually
1.
2.
3.

Others
1.
2.
3.

Example:

FUN & CONNECTION CHART

Together

Beach.
Travel.
Outdoors.
Be Present.

Individually

Read
Podcasts
Work out
Massage

Others

Dinner around the kitchen table 3 times a week.
Sunday Funday
Once a month on the boat
Pick a Day and Name it National "..." Day

CORE VALUES

Share:

Core Values Are:

- The principles, beliefs, and standards by which we live.
- The qualities we look most for in others.
- They are innate in us and govern how we live, interact, and do life.
- They shout … this is who I am … this is how I do everything.
- They are the qualities or characteristics we hold in high esteem and importance.

Ok. Based off our definitions of Core Values we want to help you identify yours. Turn to pages 22-24 to find the section on core values in your participant manual. This chart is not an exhaustive list but provides a starting place for you to find words to answer the following questions. So, choose one of the words from the list to respond to the following questions (or provide your own answer if a different word comes to mind:

1. If you could use one or two words to describe what you want to be known for … what words would you use?
2. What's a necessary quality a person must have if they want to be your friend? Or, in your relationships, what characteristic do you deem most important?
3. Think about a person who frustrates you. What quality do they lack that causes you so much irritation?
4. Think of the person you admire most; what quality do you admire about them?

The words you chose are clues to your core values. Take a moment to:

- Narrow your list of words to your top three core values, List them in the left column respectively in the his/her chart.
- Then, define what each core value means. How would you define it if you were WEBSTER'S DICTIONARY?
- Share your answers out loud.

Facilitator Note: Capture their independent answers on the Core Value chart. Then, list 2-3 of their combined core values. Capture what their core value means to them.) Here is a sample of some core values we've compiled over the years. Your participant will find them in their participant guide. ☺

Core Values List (Page 23 in their reboot workbook)

Abundance	Cooperation	Fun/Fun-loving	Kindness	Respect
Adventure	Courage	Grace/Gracious	Legacy	Results
Adaptable	Creativity	Gratitude	Love/Loving	Security
Affection	Determined	Happiness	Loyal/Loyalty	Self-development
Appreciation	Dependable	Harmony	Open-minded	Self-respect
Authenticity	Discipline	Health	Order	Self-sacrificing
Balance	Diversity	Home	Patience	Significance
Believable	Effectiveness	Honesty	Peace	Strategic
Bold	Empowerment	Honor	People	Strength
Candor	Encouragement	Hope	Positive	Success
Caring	Endurance	Humanity	Practical	Strategic
Cautious	Enjoyment	Humility	Pride	Teachable
Change	Entertainment	Humor	Professionalism	Teamwork
Clarity	Excellence	Innovation	Prosperity	Trustworthy
Companionship	Equal/Fairness	Integrity	Purposeful	Unlimited
Compassion	Faith/Faithfulness	Intelligence	Quality	Value
Connection	Family	Involvement	Quality Time	Variety
Consideration	Fitness	Impact	Reciprocity	Wealth
Consistency	Forgiveness	Intuition	Relationship	Willingness
Contentment	Freedom	Joy	Realistic	Wisdom
Contribution	Friendship	Justice	Reliable	Work Ethic

(This chart should take approximately 30-45 minutes)

OUR CORE VALUES

HIS Core Values	Define What that Core Value Means to You.
HER Core Values	**Define What that Core Value Means to You.**
OUR Core Values	**Define What that Core Value Means to You.**

Take a moment to congratulate your Couple by saying: ☺ Congratulations! You've just established one of the major building blocks to fulfilling God's Purpose, as a couple. You've identified your shared core values. Consider displaying your list of values in a place you'll see often.

Example:

OUR CORE VALUES

His Values	What that Core Value Means
Family	We share closeness and love.
Determined	We go for and get what we want in life.
Connection	We are close with the ones we love.
Her Values	**What that Core Value Means**
Faithfulness	We are fully committed.
Authenticity	We are real, genuine, and intentional.
Security	We have one another's backs.
Our Values	**What that Core Value Means**
Variety	We will live spontaneous and try new things.
Authenticity	We are real, genuine, and intentional.
Quality Time	We love connecting one on one, talking, and having fun.

MARRIAGE MOTTOS

Great job Facilitator! Isn't this fun?

Remember, TRUST THE PROCESS, and continue encouraging your Couple to LEAN IN; the BEST is yet to come!

As we continue to build on common ground to strengthen the relationship of your Couple. It's time for your Couple to create a list of the messages they want to live by as a couple.

Share:

This next chart will help you identify KEY 1-LINERS that you can use to inspire and build a strong family identity. In a sense, you can use this next chart to create mantras for your marriage and family legacy. Turn to the 50 MARRIAGE MOTTO SAMPLES provided in your participant guide on pages 25-27.

Mottos are different than core values. Rather than "innate within us," like our core values, these statements are truths we want to lean in to live by, and/or be known for!

Take a minute to circle your top 10 mottos listed from your book.

Once you have circled your top 10 let us know for the second part of your instruction.

Ok. Now take time to answer these questions to narrow your top ten in order to create your FAMILY MOTTOS:

- What are mottos you want to live by in life?
- What message or tagline inspires you to do your best?

- What catchphrases would cause you to live out your core values as a family that you'd like to make a center post to your relationships?

- Think of the exercise like this; if you created a bumper sticker for your car to capture who you are, what would it say? Or If you could share one message with the world, what would it be?

Facilitator Note: Here are the 50 MARRIAGE MOTTOS your Couple will find in their participant guide on pages 25-27.

1. Our Outcome Begins In Our Mindset
2. Concentrate Your Attention On God's Intention
3. Live Purpose-Focused, NOT Problem-Focused
4. See The Best, Believe The Best, Speak The Best
5. Prefer One Another's Needs Over Your Own
6. Make God Known. Bring God Pleasure. Demonstrate Unconditional Love
7. You Find What You Are Looking For … We Will Find What We Love, Not What Is Lacking
8. When You Can't Change How You Feel, Change The Way You Think
9. Pursue Intimacy, Not Just Sex
10. We Will Build On Common Ground & Honor One Another's Core Values
11. Envision Your Ideal Marriage And Seize It
12. Don't Settle For Good, Pursue What's Great
13. Enjoy Every Moment and Embrace The Process
14. Progress Involves Process … Do The Next Right Thing
15. What You Feed Grows … What You Starve Dies (Starve The Lies, Feed The Truth)
16. Lift The Lid … And Dare To Dream, Together
17. Release The Outcome …
18. Manage For Margin … Replenish, Together
19. Fight For, NOT With Your Spouse
20. Live Like A Tourist
21. Live, Laugh, and LOVE without reservation
22. Don't Look For The Right Partner, Be The Right Partner
23. Extend The Same Love, Acceptance, And Grace That You Need & Forgive Freely
24. Begin With The End In Mind
25. Live Intentionally To Stay Connected
26. Don't Live In The Past, Learn From It
27. Take Responsibility For Your **Own** Actions
28. We Will Be Intentional. Be Present. And Seek To Understand
29. Be A Partner, Not An Opponent & Change Your **Me** First To **We** First
30. We Gravitate Towards What We Contemplate
31. Serve, Instead Of Expecting To Be Served

32. Speak Gratitude, Not Complaints
33. Every Man Deserves To Be Valued By Their Best Moments
34. Instead Of Thinking About What You Don't Want, Think About What You Do Want
35. Remember Your Future & Dream With Your Eyes Wide Open
36. The Strength of Team is Found in its Diversity … We Will Celebrate Our Differences
37. Failing To Plan Is Planning To Fail
38. You Reap What You Sow … Plant The Right Seeds
39. Don't Allow Your *How To,* to Get In The Way Of Your *Want to*
40. Make Memories Not Madness
41. We Are Human Beings, Not Human Doings
42. Don't Let What You Don't Know, Stop You From Remembering What You Do Know.
43. Don't Let What You Can't Do, Stop You From Doing What You Can Do.
44. The Power Of Life And Death Are In The Tongue … Speak Life!
45. Who We Are Is How We Do Everything!
46. We Do What We Say And Say What We Mean
47. We Got One Another's Back
48. Live For What Matters Most
49. We Will Get It Right Within The Four Walls Of Our Home
50. Family Is Forever and Marriage Is Beautiful.

Facilitator Note: After your Couple selects their mantra/motto, document them on the next chart. Simply label the chart and bullet point 3-5 FAMILY MOTTOS your Couple chooses or creates. Instruct your Couple to identify the mottos they want to live by, especially at this point in life. Or, if they want to create something different (other than what's on the list) to feel permission to write their own.

(This chart should take approximately 30-45 minutes)

MARRIAGE & FAMILY MOTTOS
•
•
•
•
•

Example:

MARRIAGE & FAMILY MOTTOS
• Don't let what you don't know, stop you from remembering what you do know.
• Family is FOREVER & Marriage is BEAUTIFUL!
• Don't settle for GOOD things, GO for GOD things … good is the enemy of great.

LEARNING & CHECKPOINTS

As you conclude your first day together, help your couple document any learnings or checkpoints they identified throughout Day One. They should have them already captured them on separate pages throughout the day. Before you put your markers up for the day, document what they wrote.

Share: Let's document some of the learnings you documented today. What do you ALWAYS want to remember? What do you NEVER want to forget? What were some of your WOWS that was good thoughts that you'd like us to capture for your book?

How about some CHECKPOINTS?

- Remember, checkpoints are hacks that will help you change unwanted habits of what you don't want, to outcomes of what you do want. For example, we often use these words if we feel disconnected on a topic. "I may not say this right, but can I share a thought and get your help? Or … Are you at a place for us to talk; I need your help processing something? Sometimes on a funky kind of day, we might use pre-determined and agreed upon words like; Hey, I need to give you a heads up; I'm feeling off a little today …

- CHECKPOINTS specifically help answer … what can we do when this happens? Or what is a small pivot we can make to cause a better outcome? It may be something as simple as … when we feel overwhelmed, we will pause and ask; do we want to fight; or do we want to unite? Or say words like; I am listening. I hear you! How can I help?

Facilitator Note: Share any additional observations you've observed and with their permission, document your additional findings to their charts.

(This chart should take approximately 30 minutes)

The Purpose of this next chart is to document any learnings or checkpoints that they *NEVER EVER WANT TO FORGET* that will help them move forward, or that they *ALWAYS WANT TO REMEMBER*.

Learnings & Checkpoints
(We NEVER EVER WANT TO FORGET) or
(We ALWAYS WANT TO REMEMBER)
When this happens, we will do this … Or, we will say that …

1.

2.

3.

4.

5.

6.

7.

8.

9.

10.

Example:

Learnings & Checkpoints
(We NEVER EVER WANT TO FORGET) or
(We ALWAYS WANT TO REMEMBER)
When this happens, we will do this … Or, we will say that …

1. Stop defending our limitations

2. Ask, "How can they be right?"

3. Ask, "What wrong beliefs are we believing?"

4. It's either ALL GOD'S or it's NONE OF HIS

5. Are we listening through God's filters?

6. Talk about where we want to go instead of defending our emotions

7. Build on common ground—NOT our differences

8. Humility is the PROPER estimation of one's self

9. Fun is an attitude NOT an activity

10. Remember—Live inspired discipline

DAY TWO

Discover Him and Her (Page 31-31 of reboot workbook)

Open day two with a time of conversation. What thoughts did they have since yesterday? Is there anything they want to add to their learnings or checkpoints? If so, add them. If not, set the tone that today we get to begin by spending time discovering their unique gifts, and talents.

Share:

Ephesians 2:10 says that you are GOD's MASTERPIECE. And so, we want to take some time to discover each of your designs and the snowflake uniqueness you create together.

Your Purpose is NOT something you need to DO it's a celebration of WHO YOU ARE.
Your gifts and passions actually serve as a compass to discover your Purpose.

Let's get started.

Facilitator Note: Start with the Spouse that seems to need a little more prodding or probing for answers. But before you begin asking questions to discover their Purpose, encourage the other Spouse to fill in their answers as you go along, so that you can document theirs after you complete the first Spouse's. Occasionally, ask the other Spouse for input for each of their Spouse's charts to keep them focused on discovering one another.

Start with Spouse One and go through the entire chart. When you are done, re-ask the following questions to Spouse Two.

ASK:

1. What are Your Talents?
   ⇒ What are you good at? What comes natural to you? What are your gifts? What feels effortless to you? Think people (like teaching and leading) or things (like building or organizing).
2. What Inspires you to excel?
   ⇒ What causes you to do your best? What causes you to choose right over wrong? What motivates you to do your best even when no one is around? What drives you to do your best? What kind of rewards do you like?

3. What do you LOVE?
    - ⇒ What brings you joy? What would you do every single day if given the chance? What are some of your hobbies? What are you passionate about?
4. What values do you live by?
    - ⇒ What values are essential in a close friend? How would your best friend describe you? Think of someone you admire; what specifically do you admire most about them?
5. What makes you feel loved, accepted, and valued?
    - ⇒ What's your love language? What makes you feel supported? What helps to make you feel heard or understood? What makes you feel valued or respected?
6. What helps to bring you peace?
    - ⇒ Think body, mind, and soul ... what recharges you? Where do you love to travel or go? How do you find rest? What supports your overall wellbeing?
7. What is the fruit of your life?
    - ⇒ What advice or help do others seek your opinion or thoughts about; is there a recurring thing they seek your help for frequently? What do others comment about you and your gifts? What do you find yourself sharing about on a consistent basis? What are you proud of? Accomplishments?
8. At the end of life how do you want remembered?
    - ⇒ When you're in heaven, what would you want your loved ones to say or how would you want them to remember you? If you live your life well, how are others describing you at your funeral? What would the recurring comments be?

The Purpose of this next chart is to encourage and inspire your Couple that they matter! They are unique. They hold incredible Purpose. And usually takes 30-45 minutes for both charts of him and her.

DISCOVER HIM

What are Your Talents?	What Inspires You to Excel?
What do you love?	What values do you live by?
What makes you feel loved, valued, accepted?	What helps to bring you peace?
What is the fruit of your life?	At the end of life, how do you want to be remembered?

DISCOVER HER

What are Your Talents?	What Inspires You to Excel?
What do you love?	What values do you live by?
What makes you feel loved, valued, accepted?	What helps to bring you peace?
What is the fruit of your life?	At the end of life, how do you want to be remembered?

EXAMPLE:

DISCOVER HIM

What are Your Talents?	**What Inspires You to Excel?**
Connecting & discovering Managing / Leading Good Dad Problem Soving / Vision	Appreciated Accomplishment Achievement Pride In A Job Well Done

What do you love?	**What values do you live by?**
Family Faith Growth	Authenticity Moral Compass Respectful

What makes you feel loved, valued, accepted?	**What helps to bring you peace?**
Physical Touch Relationship Harmony Connection	Words Touch Lake house Worship

What is the fruit of your life?	**At the end of life, how do you want to be remembered?**
Family overcomer business leadership	He was a generous Family Man who made me feel loved, accepted, and respected.

EXAMPLE:

DISCOVER HER

What are Your Talents? Connecting Organizing Persuasion Creating & Designing	**What Inspires You to Excel?** Encouragement Appreciation Accomplishment
What do you love? Family Helping Others Posititve Growth	**What values do you live by?** Authentic Encouraging Supportive Respectful
What makes you feel loved, valued, accepted? Peaceful Household Words of afirmation Alone time	**What helps to bring you peace?** Being Outdoors Time to Design Creating Things Quiet time
What is the fruit of your life? Calm Appreciation Love Designing /Creating	**At the end of life, how do you want to be remembered?** A Kind Loving Mom who always was fun to be around

OUR MARRIAGE PURPOSE

Facilitator Note: Lead your couple to identify some of the qualities and talents they share. Chart the responses they give to the questions provided below. Also, you can pull some words over from their core values, discover charts, and even mottos to help get a feel for who they are together..

Share: We are going to create your marriage purpose together. To do that, let me ask you some questions. We'll document your answers under the headings of NOUNS. VERBS. AND DESCRIPTIVES. Here we go.

1. What are some common talents you share?
2. What projects do you enjoy doing together?
3. What kind of people do you both enjoy being around, or helping?
4. If you could only accomplish one thing in life together, what would you do?
5. When people walk away after spending time with the two of you together, how do you want them to feel?
6. If you could choose to work with people or things, which would you choose?
7. What kind of hobbies do you both enjoy?
8. What feels effortless; like, even though it's work, it feels like play?
9. Describe a time the two of you felt the most joy and fulfillment working or playing together. What were you doing? Who were you with? What kind of qualities did those people share?
10. What common themes emerge from your discover charts?
11. What are your shared or complimentary core values?
12. How would you finish the following statements?
    a. We live to …

b. We love to …

c. We are passionate about …

d. We won't stop until we …

e. The one thing we believe God wants us to do is …

Facilitator Note: Create two separate statements based on their answers and your observation. Your client can create their own purpose statement, or wordsmith the statement you created. If you have a couple who wants to create their own or is hesitant to commit to either of the statements that you created, help them craft their own marriage purpose by utilizing their answers to the questions below. Use the chart on the next page to capture their answers to the questions you ask.

(This chart should take approximately 30-45 minutes)

Facilitator Note: The Purpose of this chart is to capture your Couple's unique qualities and help them land on their MARRIAGE PURPOSE. List their answers in the appropriate columns.

OUR MARRIAGE PURPOSE

Nouns	Verbs	Descriptives

OPTION ONE: We exist to …

_____

_____

OPTION TWO: We exist to …

_____

_____

FINAL REVISION: We exist to …

_____

_____

Examples of Purpose Statements from previous MARRIAGE REBOOT RETREATS:

1. We exist to lead a godly family on the cornerstones of grace, love, and acceptance.
2. We exist to reveal the kingdom of God through the ministry of the Holy Spirit.
3. We exist to encourage and inspire other's value and worth.
4. We exist to create an environment of acceptance, loyalty, trust, and God's love to people.
5. We are a fun, loving, adventurous family demonstrating responsibility, unconditional love, and positivity.
6. We exist to impact relationships through righteous, joyful, & authentic connection.
7. We exist to create environments of RESPECT, PERSEVERANCE, TRUST, AND LOVE.
8. We were designed to LOVE, LEAD, and SERVE to encourage independence and value.
9. We steward God's abundance and peace to empower others to thrive.
10. We exist to provide pathways to sustainable growth and life transformation.
11. We exist to create content that inspires life transformation.
12. We exist to demonstrate unconditional love and honor to our family and encourage others.
13. We create a legacy of encouragement, trust, validation, and unconditional love in family.
14. We exist to impact lives by making the complex simple.
15. We exist to empower leaders to maximize their vision and Purpose.
16. We exist to serve as a godly example of leadership and service to others.
17. We exist to encourage our family and others to grow and experience God's Love.
18. We exist to facilitate change and growth.
19. We exist to create an environment of faith, belief, joy, and peace.
20. We exist to influence Kingdom-minded couples to unify and connect with genuine love.
21. We encourage and empower people to have hope and walk in truth.
22. As faith-filled overcomers, we encourage authentic, joyful, drama-free living.
23. We exist to create lifegiving peaceful environments of grace and authenticity.
24. We provide environments that help people feel comfortable, valued, and to thrive.
25. As overcomers, we encourage and inspire others through our family, giving and faithfulness.

Facilitator Note: At this place in your facilitation, it's time to help your Couple move from where they are to where they REALLY want to be, by creating a vision for their future.

OUR MARRIAGE VISION (Page 37-38 of their marriage reboot workbook)

Share:

This next chart marks a shift in your MARRIAGE REBOOT RETREAT. We are moving from where we are and from gaining awareness, into where you really want to be and creating a vision for your future.

Did you know you can remember your future? We know, it sounds weird but think of it this way.

GOD is not bound by time or space. We are bound by the continuum of time and space… but GOD sees the beginning from to the end simultaneous.

Ecclesiastes 3: 14-15: I know that there is nothing better for them than to rejoice and to do good in one's lifetime; moreover, that every man who eats and drinks sees good in all his labor—it is the gift of God. I know that everything God does will remain forever; there is nothing to add to it and there is nothing to take from it, for God has *so* worked that men should fear Him. **That which is has been already** and that **which will be, has already been**, for God seeks what has passed by.[ii]

God has seen your life from beginning to end. Before you were born, He knew your beginning, and your last day. (Jeremiah 1:5, Psalm 139:16) He is not bound by time or space. (Psalm 90:2, Psalm 139:7-10, Revelation1:8) And now think of this. His Spirit according to Scripture searches the mind of God. (1 Corinthians 2:10-11) And, THE HOLY SPIRIT, the same Spirit that raise Christ from the dead, lives in us. (Romans 8:11) Therefore, that same spirit that searches the mind of GOD that lives in us, can help us search and know the mind of GOD. The same God that sees time from beginning to end. We can know and see our future.

Here's another way of thinking about the power of vision and imagination.

- ☐ The chair you are sitting in once only existed in someone's mind as an imagination or vision.

- ☐ Athletes frequently leverage their imagination of the perfect vision: perfect pass, perfect free throw, perfect jump, etc.

So, here are some Questions to consider to welcome GOD'S PERFECT VISION.

1. First and foremost, what do you want? Take a moment to list 2 or 3 things you desire in each of your life domains. Look back at your Where We Want to Be Chart. If you were living them, what would your life look like 2 years from today?
2. What would the two of *you* attempt to do *if you knew you wouldn't fail*?
3. What future picture energizes your mind, will and emotion? What vision empowers you to do everything possible to achieve it?
4. What dream serves your Purpose and calls out your potential as a couple?
5. What seeds possibility in your soul and calls you to pursue life together?
6. What would you do if you had no limitations?
7. What would you do if you had unlimited resources?
8. In your most perfect vision ... what are you doing together?
9. Is there anything you would change if you knew you only had five years to live?"
10. What do you believe God's vision is for your marriage?

Facilitator Note: Before you have your Couple create their vision, share your recorded 2–3-minute Vision Video. OR to cast this portion of the REBOOT PROCESS, PLAY SESSION 7 from the DISCOVER YOUR MARRIAGE PURPOSE COURSE ~ VISION fuels YOUR Purpose! As you get started, remind your couple:

- REMEMBER your FUTURE.

- This is NOT a GOAL chart ... we are not trying to say, we are here, and we want to get there ... instead ... visualize your future with GOD's help. Illustrate your vision by stating "we are" rather than," we will" or "we want to" or we intend to."

- Quiet yourself and invite Him to help you see from the place of … we are here. This has happened. Stay in that vision and feel what it feels like.

- The "how loop" is a loop because it's never ending. We limit our vision if we worry or try to figure out **HOW**…Avoid getting stuck in the *how-loop* by get a clear picture of your future environment and instead of asking *how do we get there?* Begin to ask yourself; how did we get *here*? Keep your future in PRESENT TENSE by asking; what are we enjoying? What are we experiencing? How does it feel? How are you living with spontaneity? How are you enjoying a new rhythm of life? How are you leaning into God's Best? How have you bridged the gap with others and one another? How is your FUN meter reading? What's your finances and health like? How about your communication? How are you enjoying one another?

Facilitator Note: Instruct your Couple to **individually** write two sentences that capture their vision for each of the areas of their life: lifestyle of health and finances, marriage/family, career/calling, faith and extended relationships. When they finish, invite them to each share what they wrote. Then as a facilitator, chart their combined vision.

(This chart should take approximately 1 ½ hours)

OUR MARRIAGE VISION (Page 37 or marriage reboot workbook)

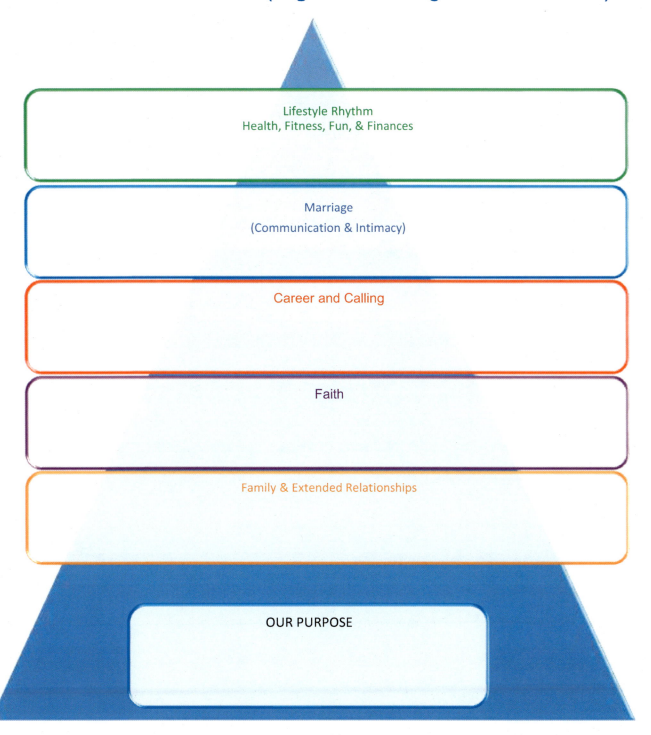

Instruct your Couple to write 2 sentences for each of the domains listed above, and to use words in the present tense of what they truly envision; words like WE ARE … NOT … WE WILL. Also, have them fill in their 12 word or less combined purpose statement.

Lifestyle Rhythm
Health, Fitness, Fun, & Finances

We are thriving empty nesters who live a healthy, active lifestyle with like-minded, growth-oriented friends. We enjoy weekend trips to our beachfront home that also provides revenue to support our lifestyle. We seek weekly adventure getaways.

Marriage
(Communication & Intimacy

We anticipate one another's needs. We are curious on how to serve each other in all dimensions of intimacy. We are more in love than ever before.

Career and Calling

We consistently build into the lives of 1,000s of individuals and married couples by providing resources, content, and coaching, and helping them create significant lives. We actively serve at CF in roles where we help team members move forward in individual leadership, while at the same time regularly speaking at churches around the world and coaching individuals / couples in marriage and executive leadership. We coach and equip church leaders, providing wisdom in a safe place for ministry leaders.

Faith

We love experiencing our depth of communication with God through the Holy Spirit. Our life circumstances disciple us and grow us closer to God.

Family & Extended Relationships

We love family vacations every year. Our adult children seek our advice and wisdom. We love spending time together as a family.

PURPOSE

We build and empower people to create significant lives.

Manage for What's Best!

The Purpose of this next chart is to help your Couple Manage for What's Best!

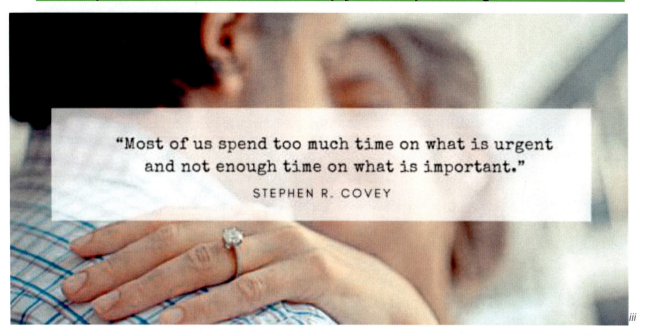

Share: What you feed grows and what you starve dies. So, let's determine the seeds we want to plant and water. And discern the weeds that will threaten God's Purpose for your marriage so we can remove them. This next chart provides a place for us to capture the **Things You Need to Manage For & The Things You Need to Manage Against.** Think of it this way:

- The things we need to manage for are the things we catch ourselves saying; I'm going to... I meant to... I was going to ... but for some reason they always seem to slip through the cracks. They are the seeds of our life that need planted and watered to grow us toward our desired goals. If we fail to 'manage for' them, they get crowded out by life's busyness. We need to manage for these things.
- The things we *manage against* are hazardous habits that deter us from living our ideal marriage. They are weeds needing pulled. If we fail to 'manage *against*' these practices, habits, or faulty beliefs, we tend to get out of a healthy life rhythm and feel defeated. Keep in mind, at first glance some weeds may appear harmless, but in the end, they keep us in our comfort zone and rob us of God's best. (Like timewasters such as social media or unnecessary activities that steal our time from connection.)

- The things we need to manage against are the things that trip us up, they are the recurring themes or situations that throw us off course and cause us to lose the battle.
- We need to set up the proper boundaries and know how we will respond to win the battle and take ground. Think about your marriage purpose. What decisions or changes do you need to make to ensure you fulfill it, as a couple? Let's list the things you need to 'manage for' and things you need to 'manage against' to live your marriage vision.
- Let's pause to consider what do you need to manage for and what do you need to manage against in the individual aspects of your marriage?

Facilitator Note: Use the following questions (as needed) to fill in their chart for each domain of their life:

1. What practices will help produce favorable results?
2. What actions do you need to take, to help produce your desired outcome?
3. What habits threaten your desired outcome?
4. What could lead you off course or distract you from fulfilling your marriage purpose?
5. How can you safeguard what matters most?
6. What habits will help you succeed?
7. What daily and weekly practices do you need to establish to defend your Purpose?
8. What intentional habits can you develop to move you toward your Purpose?
9. Is there anything you need to REMOVE from your life to live your vision?
10. Is there anything you need to ADD to live your vision?

(This chart should take approximately 30-45 minutes.)

Things to Manage For / Things to Manage Against

Things to Manage For	Things to Manage Against
LIFESTYLE RHYTHM (Health, Fitness, Fun & Finances)	LIFESTYLE RHYTHM (Health, Fitness, Fun & Finances)
MARRIAGE Communication & Intimacy	MARRIAGE Communication & Intimacy
FAITH	FAITH
CAREER / CALLING	CAREER / CALLING
FAMILY & EXTENDED RELATIONSHIPS	FAMILY & EXTENDED RELATIONSHIPS

Things to Manage For / Things to Manage Against

Things to Manage For	Things to Manage Against
BEING PRESENT and PLANNING FUN	NOT SPENDING FRIVOUSLY
EMOTIONAL CONNECTION. SPEAK LIFE.	TIME WASTERS – SOCIAL MEDIA – LETTING THE KIDS RULE OUR SCHEDULE – THROW OUT THE SCOREBOARD
PRAYING TOGETHER	JUDGEMENT-Unforgiveness-Feeling Less Than My Partner
MUTUAL SUPPORT and ENCOURAGEMENT	MINIMIZING OUR PRGGRESS
ESTABLISH HEALTHY BOUNDARIES for kids and the in-laws. PUT ONE ANOTHER FIRST.	People pleasing for fear of backlash if we don't do things the way other want us to (both our kids and our in-laws)

This optional chart should take 15 – 30 minutes.

Facilitator Note: The Purpose of this next chart is to get rid of activities that crowd room for connection or crowd our margin so we can't focus on our priority and vision.

Share: What activities, time suckers or obligations do you have that you need to eliminate to add margin into your life? Look back on your past couple of weeks and consider, what do I need to let go of? What are time wasters? What do I do out of a sense of obligation that move me away from our vision or eat up my time? What energy drains can I dump? Is there anything that can be delegated? What's good but NOT great? What is unnecessary or not lifegiving? Specifically in relation to TIME/SELF management.

What do you need to get rid of to make room for more of those kinds of activities?

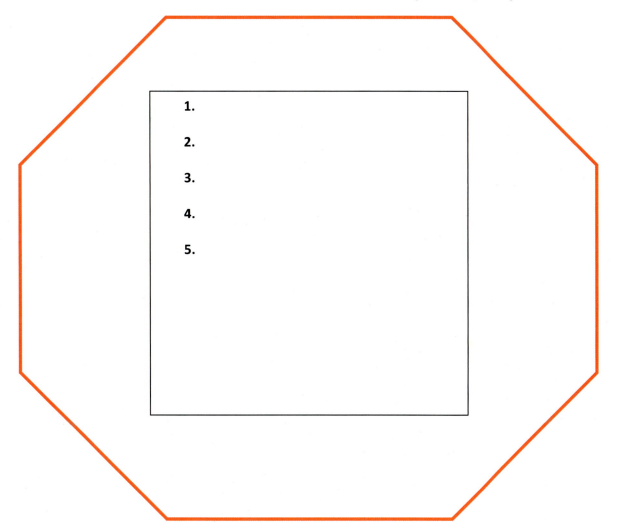

STOP DOING CHART (sample)

1. Time Wasters

2. Excessive phone time

3. Being Available

4. Too much TV

5. Saying YES too much

WHAT'S NEXT CHART
WHERE DO WE GO FROM HERE?

Facilitator Note:

The Purpose of this next chart is to determine a small actionable step and put a timeline to it to move forward to the desired outcome and vision.

As you create this FINAL chart, refer to your Couple's Where We Want to Be Chart and their Vision Chart. Help them work through an actionable plan to move forward by identifying THE PRIORITY for each aspect of their marriage relationship ant the steps they need to take.

As they respond, combine what they documented from their WHERE WE WANT TO BE chart and what they created together from their vision. List in a simplistic way what their DESIRED OUTCOME is, in the left-hand Column.

In the next Column, list the specific action of what they identified as TOP PRIORITY.

And, in the third column list the frequency of days or specific dates they will complete or begin that step.

Share:

Want to and Follow through are two different things altogether. So, it's time to create some practical steps to live out the qualities and learnings you've identified over the past couple of days. We are NOW at the FINAL planning phase for living out the VISION and DESIRED OUTCOME you desire for your life and marriage.

It's important to **create a DO-ABLE plan that helps you move toward your Desired Outcome.**

As we create this chart, it's important to identify S.M.A.R.T. goals. S.M.A.R.T. goals are:

➢ Small / Specific

- Measurable
- Attainable / Achievable
- Realistic / Relevant
- Time sensitive in nature / Time Bound

Briefly describe each section by saying:

We are going to begin by listing (in the first column) what you desire. We will combine what you listed initially in the WHERE WE WANT TO BE CHART, with the vision you created, and bullet point in a singular sentence what you desire most, right now, in each aspect of your marriage relationship.

In the WHAT'S MY PART (HIM/HER) Section, we will list what YOU need to do to ensure that you support what you both decided you want. We'll ask you some specific questions to help you discern things you need to do, change, or new habits you need to create to support what you want to experience for each aspect of your marriage relationship.

In the last section we will identify the #1 PRIORITY that you need to focus on and the action step you will take, and WHEN you will implement it.

For the Non-Negotiable section it's important to remember that in order for us to experience our vision, we need to live intentionally, unwrite any vows we've lived by that compromise GOD's VISION and PURPOSE for our marriage and life, and establish NEW RULES for living. We often hear in marriage that we should never use the words always or never … but in this case … let's try to establish some we will always or we will never to provide new habits and new ways of thinking that we want to live by.

The last section is OUR PRIORITY. We want to encourage you to ask one another daily or at least once a week; "What's THE PRIORITY for us this week? Even if we don't accomplish anything else; if we accomplish this ONE thing, we will be happy and feel like we are moving forward?"

OK. Let's dive in!

Let's start with Marriage. As you look at you WHERE WE WANT TO BE CHART and YOUR VISION, what is the number one thing right now that you desire most as it pertains to your relationship, your communication and/or your intimacy?

(Facilitator, go to the next section linear and in the WHAT'S MY PART HIM/HER section have your Couple reflect to their response of what they say they want most for this area.)

From your perspective what do you feel your individual part is to ensure your desired outcome?

Facilitator, you may ask them …

- What do they need to do?
- What do they need to change?
- What do they need to welcome, to move toward their desired outcome?
- You can use questions like: what do you need to do in this specific area to ensure you help to ensure your desired outcome?
- What do you need to change to support what you agree is important?
- How can you help to build on common ground and live toward what you both desire?
- What is one way you can live intentionally to live your vision and marriage purpose?

Next as you move linear, remind your couple of what a NON-NEGOTIALBE IS by saying …

Ok, as we continue to move linear on the chart. You've both identified what you desire together, and what each of your individual parts are; let's establish a NEW NON-NEGOTIABLE that you can live by. Remember,

- Non-negotiables are not open for discussion. They are fixed, set, and firm.
- They are the lines in the sand, that will NOT be crossed.
- They are the standards we will NOT deviate.
- Non-negotiables are the WE WILL ALWAYS … or … WE WILL NEVER … statements that a couple is NOT willing to compromise.

Are there any NEW VOWS you ant to make to replace faulty beliefs or new rules you want to implement to secure your desired outcome?

(Ok Facilitator … last section)

Share: You guys are doing great.

Also, as we identify your #1 priority for each aspect of your marriage let's also determine a timeline to your S.M.A.R.T. goal so that you can not only decide what the next step is but you can put a timeframe around it to help you put action toward what you both want together.

(This chart should take 1-1 ½ hours)

WHAT'S NEXT CHART

Category	What We Want (Desired Outcome)	His Part	Her Part	Non-negotiable	Our Priority The Next Step We Will Take … And, when?
Marriage — Communication & Intimacy					
Lifestyle Rhythm — Health, Fitness, Fun, & Finances					
Career / Calling					
Faith					
Family / Extended Relationship					
What is one way that your spouse can support you?					

WHAT'S NEXT CHART

Category	What We Want (Desired Outcome)	His Part	Her Part	Non-negotiable	Our Priority — The Next Step We Will Take … And, when?
Marriage — Communication & Intimacy	We desire deeper intimacy and vulnerable connection.	Honesty and Vulnerable communication in temptations and failures.	Communicate And Extend Unconditional Love	We will always be vulnerable and express unconditional love.	Prayer daily and during that time ask for the heart check 10-1-21
Lifestyle Rhythm — Health, Fitness, Fun, & Finances	We want to travel, buy properties and explore together.	Eliminated debt and continue making money	Eliminate debt and continue making money	We won't bring on new consumer debt.	Write out our future goals. 10-27-21
Career / Calling	We want to help couples in marriage and family	Praying into the vision and building relationships	Travel with Brian as often as possible	We will always honor our relationship first and foremost.	Hold certification conversation with Greg & Julie 10-18-21
Faith	We want to experience God's presence and to experience a like-minded group of people	Get quiet with God	Seek Community and continued growth	We will release the outcome and find contentment in HIS timeline.	Seek Community and Accountability 10-15-21
Family / Extended Relation-ship	We desire to help and prepare families and marriages realize their potential and purpose	Build our relationship and demonstrate respect in leading our family	Spend quality time with the kids	We will fight for unity above all else	Define our house rules and post them 11-1-21
Spouse: What would you say is the greatest need?		Be honest even when it's not easy	Verbalize unconditional love		

Congratulations, facilitator! You have completed your facilitation!

Diffuse the Bombs in Your Marriage
(Build On Common Ground)

1. Create the Optimal Environment for Unity
   - Discuss in a neutral place / space of mind
   - Delay having a conversation when you are tired, overly frustrated, feeling irrational, or easily offendable
   - Avoid judgment, accusations, or hearing from a place of woundedness
2. Build on Common Ground
   - Discover what you both agree you want. Keep at a high level when necessary.
   - Be objective toward your combined desired outcome
3. Fight for Unity Above All Else
   - Listen with an open mind
     - How could they be right?
     - What do you agree with, with what they are saying?
- Affirm what you agree with…
   - "I totally get that…"
   - "I couldn't agree more…"
   - "Absolutely understand that…"
   - Listen for understanding, not reply. Ask questions!
   - Create an environment where your spouse feels listened to, heard, and understood.

*When you cannot do these steps or feel stuck…get a coach!

3 Ways To Stay Connected- Body, Mind, & Soul

1. Be intentional, daily. Remember the beginnings? Date night?
    a. Prepare and look your best.
    b. Put your best foot forward.
2. Live to discover one another.
    a. Plan conversations. Think about things to talk about. (Conversation starters.)
    b. Daily, think of expressing one thing you love and admire about your spouse. Look for what you love about them. Not what is lacking.
3. Look for opportunities to laugh and rest together.
    a. On a weekly basis, plan a place and time to rest.
    b. Put on your listening ears and look for ways to agree and build on common ground.
    c. Change up the scenery and intentionally turn off the electronics.

Now apply those 3 ways to stay connected and think … BODY-MIND-SOUL

Parenting Principles for Every Season

Every season of parenting requires intentionality, adaptation, and change. No matter the season here are some of the principles we've learned and are learning –

1. **We must adapt to the season and transition well.** Your role as parent must change there is no cookie cutter –
    a. At every season of life, we like to ask: What does love require?
    b. As toddlers, it requires consistency. Laying the ground work.
    c. As young: We play the role of coach and help them test what they've learned.
    d. As adults: We must parent from influence of adult to adult. We need to love them enough to let them go (our role must change) be encourage not intrusive not invited or welcomed encourage and supporting affirm vs advise express only what you love and affirm

2. **Establish connection build relationship.**
    a. GREAT BP: Think of your friendships: Friends hold Conversations and tell stories, share dreams, share ideas, confess worries, give hope and encouragement, ask questions, listen. The same principles that govern your friendships, work with building relationship within the family.
    b. Don't say everything you think
    c. Don't fix em
    d. Give respect
    e. Sincere apologies
    f. Have serious fun-play together - fun factor - fun experience
    g. Make Memories.
    h. **As teens: Rules without relationship breeds rebellion.**
    i. **As adults:** Welcome the New Role reinvent the new relationship. Be a coach - help transition to successful adult (your thoughts on that and their thoughts) be there biggest support mentors don't push they listen and move at the pace of given influence … be patient and believe the best. Encourage independence … let them learn
    j. At every level of parenting: Be caring but not enabling
    k. Leave legacy build intentional memories
    l. Live w no regrets God and family
    m. Prayer

3. **Ask questions:** Find out what they think. Ask open-ended question. Talk with … not at

    a. What do they dream about? What do they desire?
    b. Who do they want to become/be?
    c. What do you think? what do you need from me? How can I support you?

4. **Whenever possible … Speak life.** Speak words of unmerited Grace. Every person longs to be loved accepted and valued. Your are loved. You are accepted. You are valued. I believe in you. I know you will choose the right mate. Demonstrate AWE- Affection warmth and encouragement for your children

5. **Release the outcome … let go of the unrealistic and welcome the new future**

    a. The idea of control
    b. The idea of perfection
    c. The idea of spare them from every pain and heartache. You can't always alleviate pain or hardship
    d. Let go of control - their finances, relationships, choices, their vision
    e. Let go of expectations and timelines
    f. Grieve what's loss … let go of the past season …

6. You can't give what you ain't got. Invest in your own emotional physical and spiritual health (your own oxygen)

7. Walk in unity with your spouse.

    a. No room for blame
    b. Decide what's important that you both agree on.
    c. Determine your family rhythm for intentional one on one connection with each other and with the family connection.
    d. Decide on parenting principles and the individuality of influence for each child.
    e. Choose to not be offended
    f. Don't parent out of guilt

How to Know When to Say Yes and No

When We Say YES!

1. GOD says YES. ☺
2. It aligns with our vision and calling to RESTORE FAMILY.
3. We can make a significant impact to advance the kingdom.
4. We can grow and learn.
5. It moves the needle financially / spiritually / relationally.
6. We are excited about it.
7. We love the people who are leading it and want to build relationship with them.
8. The people who are involved love us.
9. We feel Celebrated.
10. And, when we bring life, it's reflected back to us in appreciation.

WHEN WE ABSOLUTELY SAY NO!

1. When we are NOT in agreement.
2. We say no, when it distracts us from our vision.
3. We say no, when it steals our energy.

QUESTIONS TO CONSIDER

1. Does it work well with our other commitments both now and projected vision? Does it align with the season we are in NOW and add value to our call to advance the kingdom?
2. Is there a HUGE HECK YES … this is exciting in our hearts?
3. Do we love the people who are leading it or participating in it?
4. Will it move the needle in impact and propel us forward with measurable results?
5. Will we hone a skill and get 'practice' by participating or grow and learn by being involved?
6. Do we feel celebrated by the people involved?
7. Are we in agreement?

Conversation Starters

1. As a kid, what'd you do for fun that you'd love to do again?
2. What is your favorite childhood memory?
3. What kind of person were you in high school?
4. Who positively influenced your life the most?
5. What's right; what are you celebrating in life?
6. What's wrong; what would you like to change about your life?
7. What's missing; what would be life feel more fulfilling if you could add it to your life?
8. What feels confused in your life, right now, that you'd like to gain clarity?
9. When did you experience God's love? When did He seem the most real to you?
10. What three words best describe me?
11. What are you celebrating the most, right now, in life?
12. What do you look forward to?
13. What do you like to do to relax after a long day of work?
14. In a single word, how would you answer this question: If you could add one thing to your life right now, what would it be? And, why … what would it provide that is currently missing?
15. What do you believe God's vision is for us as a couple?
16. What do you want to be remembered for?
17. If you could share one essential message with the world, what would your message be?
18. Describe a time on where you felt the most alive and joyful in marriage.
19. What is your favorite date with your spouse and what made it so great?
20. If we could go on a date and money wasn't an issue, what would you do?
21. If we went on a day trip together, where would you go, what would you do?
22. If you could have any gift right now under $100 what would it be?
23. What makes a date feel successful to you?
24. What's your favorite story you love telling about me?
25. Tell me a secret.
26. What are some creative ways we can pay ourselves first, in money and time, to secure our future?
27. What's one of your favorite attributes that you really love or respect about your spouse?
28. What quality do you appreciate most in a person?
29. What causes you to feel appreciated?
30. What causes you to feel dishonored, devalued or disrespected?
31. If you could have a conversation with anyone, living or dead, who would you choose and why?
32. Complete this sentence: I love how you _____ I wish I were more like that.
33. If they made a movie about us, which actor or actress would play your part? Which would play mine?
34. If you could spend the day with a famous celebrity, who would you hang with?
35. Who was your favorite teacher and why?
36. What one trait do you admire about your dad?
37. What trait do you most admire about your mom?

38. What is our desire outcome in (parenting, marriage, finances, spiritual growth, sexual intimacy)?
39. What did you learn about marriage from your upbringing?
40. If you could change one thing about your circumstances, what would it be? Are there any steps you can take to begin embracing that change?
41. Who was your best friend growing up? What made them so special?
42. If you could take two weeks off of work, what would you do?
43. What is your favorite holiday and why?
44. What was your favorite holiday tradition growing up?
45. What's a family tradition you want to repeat?
46. What did your parents do that you never want to repeat?
47. What was you most memorable birthday? What made it so memorable?
48. How can we use our combined gifts to bring God pleasure?
49. What is your favorite scripture?
50. When do you feel the closest to God?
51. When do you feel the closest to me?
52. What makes you feel safe?
53. How can I pray for you this week?
54. When have you laughed so hard you cried?
55. What is your idea of an ideal vacation?
56. What one place would you like to go on a vacation too?
57. What are the most enjoyable things you love doing with me?
58. Who do you most enjoy being around?
59. Whom do you naturally find yourself reaching out to?
60. Whom do you/we most enjoy being around?
61. Whom do you enjoy helping?
62. If you shared a message with the world, what would that message be?
63. How can we serve God and one another specifically this week?
64. What childhood memory do you wish you could relive?
65. If you could be mentored by anyone, who would it be and why?
66. What's your favorite song of all time?
67. What's your high of the day? What's your low?
68. If you could test drive or buy any kind of car what would it be?
69. What's your favorite amusement park experience? Roller coaster?
70. If you could live anywhere, where would it be?
71. If you could be the star in a reality series, or a tv drama, what would it be?
72. What's dish do you like to prepare? What's your favorite thing to cook?
73. Who's your favorite superhero, and why?
74. If you could have any super hero power, what would it be?
75. If you could hire a maid, a chef, or a personal massage therapist every day, which would you hire?
76. When you're stressed, what helps you relax?
77. What's the best thing that's happened to you, or for you, lately?
78. When do you feel most loved by me?
79. What about me makes you smile?
80. What mottos do you live by?

81. What quotes inspire you?
82. What statements capture who you are in any given day?
83. If you created a bumper sticker for who you are, what would it say?
84. If we could create a bumper sticker for our marriage, how would it read?
85. What did we do when we first dated that you'd like to do again?
86. How can we expand our influence?
87. Are the thoughts your thinking and decisions you making --planting the right seeds for your desired harvest?
88. What are you doing right now that will help yield a favorable result?
89. What actions do you need to take today to help produces your desired outcome?
90. Are there any habits threatening your desired outcome that need to be uprooted and gotten rid of?
91. If you could travel to any place in the world, where would you go and why?
92. What do you believe God wants us to believe for?
93. Is there anyway we are living limited to our abilities that God wants us to believe for HIS capabilities?
94. What one way do you want to grow in this year?
95. What changes do we need to make to better welcome our ideal marriage?
96. What are 3 practical ways you will live to grow this month?
97. Have you/we given up on a dream because it didn't happen in our timeline that we need to believe for again?
98. How can we align our thinking with God's to better celebrate life and one another?
99. How can I serve you this week that would cause you to feel more valued?
100. Who's your favorite actor/actress?
101. What one fact do I not know about you?
102. How can we believer for BIGGER things?
103. What keeps us from dreaming together?
104. Is the glass half-empty or half-full?
105. What's your natural tendency; do you live to solve problems or pursue purpose?
106. What's your biggest pet peeve?
107. How can we better laugh, love and live life to its fullest?
108. What needs to be in place for you to enjoy living life to its fullest?
109. What do you love to do?
110. What feels like you're playing even though you're working?
111. If you could go back to your childhood and learn to play one instrument, what would it be?
112. If you could go back to your childhood and learn to master any one thing what would it be?
113. I love how you _____ because that's a weakness of mine.
114. What's your biggest fear?
115. What causes you anxiety or stress?
116. Does a fear of failing ever cause you to stop from stepping out to serve God?
117. What is your most favorite attribute you enjoy about me?
118. How have I helped you grow?
119. How do our differences add dimension to our marriage?
120. How do our differences harmonize to maximize our efforts?

121. How do our differences make us stronger?
122. What are some way we can intentionally defer to one another's strengths?
123. How can we better operate as partners vs opponents?
124. How can we better celebrate NOT just tolerate one another and demonstrate appreciation?
125. What's the number one thing on your bucket list?
126. If you knew you only had a few years to live, would you live differently? If so, how? What would you change?
127. What makes you know (feel) that I welcome your perspective and insights?
128. What Scripture seems the most pertinent to you in this season of life?
129. As you reflect on life, what caused you to grow the most?
130. On a scale of 1-10 how satisfied do you feel in life; what would move you closer to the 10?
131. What area do you feel you are growing the most in during this season of life?
132. What are you celebrating the most during this season of life?
133. How can we better enjoy every moment, and embrace life to it's fullest?
134. What do we want our future to look like? What practical steps can we take to move toward it?
135. How can we better welcome our differences and even celebrate them?
136. In potentially divisive areas what do we agree on?
137. What activities foster connection and unity in our home, within our family?
138. What activities can we put into practice to help us achieve our dreams together?
139. How can we live to bring pleasure to one another and joy each day?
140. In what areas are we most thriving as a couple?
141. What quality do you admire most about me physically, emotionally, intellectually and spiritually?
142. If you could describe our marriage, how would you describe it in 5 words or less?
143. What are some one-liner principles you live by?
144. How do we inspire greatness, together?
145. What inspires you to be your best?
146. As a couple, what inspires us?
147. What fills us with passion?
148. How are our talents and gifts similar?
149. What similar passions do we share?
150. Together, who do we most care about?
151. What are you most grateful for in life?
152. This week, what do we need to make time for?
153. What disciplines do we need to apply to our daily efforts to secure our greatest success as a couple?
154. What replenishes you physically?
155. What replenishes you intellectually?
156. What replenishes you emotionally?
157. What replenishes you spiritually?
158. What do you admire most about me?
159. Which do you prefer spoken affirmation or written affirmation?

160. What's your love language? Words of affirmation, Physical touch? Gifts? Works of service? Or, quality time?
161. What are you most proud about accomplishing?
162. How can we better invite God's presence into our marriage and home?
163. How does God want us to grow so that we can better welcome His purpose for our life and marriage?
164. What do we need to let go of in order to live life to its fullest this week?
165. What's the craziest thing God's ever asked you to do?
166. What's the most personal way God's ever spoke to you?
167. What helps you embrace "what is" while you press forward to "what is yet to be"?
168. If you were stranded on a desert island, what 5 things would you want to have with you?
169. What are 3-5 essentials of life that bring you the most joy?
170. When have you felt the most successful?
171. What three things do you treasure most in life?
172. What's your favorite Christmas memory?
173. What's your favorite memory of your mom?
174. What's your favorite memory of your dad?
175. What's your favorite memory of your grandparent(s)?
176. What's your favorite Thanksgiving food?
177. What's your favorite dessert?
178. What helps you to renew your mind?
179. What helps you renew your body?
180. What helps you renew your soul?
181. What is your most favorite thing that I have ever done for you?
182. What do you love most about our relationship?
183. What is the hardest thing you ever had to do?
184. What is the greatest thing you've ever achieved?
185. What's the best gift /present you ever received?
186. How do our different perspectives add wisdom and depth to our marriage?
187. What practical ways can we better demonstrate love and respect for each other?
188. If we were tourists visiting this area, what activities would we do? What places would we visit?
189. What do you dream about?
190. When do you feel the most valued by me?
191. What is your most favorite thing I have ever done for you?
192. What do you like best about our relationship?
193. Which of my attributes do you find the most attractive?
194. What steps does God desire for us to take together in faith?
195. What practical steps can we take to begin embracing God purpose for our marriage?
196. What's your favorite book? Why did you like it? What did you learn?
197. Imagine you're 90 years old sitting on your favorite chair, overlooking your favorite view, what are you celebrating about life's experience? What are you glad you lived for?
198. What Next steps has God already spoken to you that you have not yet taken action on?

199. What is one of your darkest seasons of life; what did it teach you; how did you grow because of it?
200. What reoccurring thought do you battle?
201. Describe what retirement looks like for you?
202. What does financial freedom look like to you? Describe it as vividly as you can.
203. Finish this sentence by filling in the blanks. If I could _____, I would _____.
204. What gifts has God given you and how can you use them creatively for Him?
205. How has God demonstrated His unconditional love to you?
206. How would you describe yourself in three words?
207. If you could change and grow one way physically, what would it be and why?
208. So often we get stuck in the GOT-to's of life that we forget the GET-to's; what is a "GET TO" that you want to safeguard and do more often?
209. What activities do we need to prioritize?
210. What pursuits align with God's purpose for our marriage that we need to make more room for?
211. What activities bring us the most fulfillment as a couple?
212. What sabotages your dreams that we can manage against, together?
213. What are your biggest money-makers?
214. What are your greatest strengths and how can you better leverage them?
215. What are three of my greatest strengths?
216. When you're fatigued, what motivates you to keep pressing on and to do your best?
217. How can we utilize our talents right now, where we are now?
218. What are you the most excited about concerning our future, together?
219. What does success look like to you?
220. What do we want for our marriage?
221. In our most perfect vision, what does our ideal marriage relationship look like?
222. What is GOD'S idea of an ideal marriage look like for us?
223. Using your imagination, where are we living, what are we doing, and what does our ideal life look like 5 years from now?
224. What are we doing well at?
225. What do we need to improve?
226. Where do we need to grow?
227. Does it come easier to write your thoughts, or verbalize your thoughts?
228. What are some common interests we share that we love to do together?
229. What do you find as your biggest time wasters; is there someone you could delegate or higher out those tasks to who find them in their wheelhouse?
230. What do you think about _____?
231. What's a fun activity/recreation that you'd enjoy doing more often?
232. Is there anywhere in life you feel you need more balance?
233. At the end of the day, what makes it feel complete and fulfilled?
234. Where do you feel like you've made the most progress in life?
235. What's on your bucket list?
236. If you could do one thing right now, what would it be?
237. If you could fly, where would you fly to?
238. If you could be invisible, who would you spy on and why?

239. What's your most embarrassing moment?
240. What motivates you to do your best?
241. What do you need to release to God? What is God speaking for you to do? How is He asking you to serve?
242. What causes you to retreat or pull back from your dreams?
243. What is something that's really important to you this week to accomplish? How can I support you? How can I hold you accountable? How can I help you achieve your goals?
244. Who else can help us achieve our dreams?
245. How do you want to live intentional in parenting this week?
246. How do you want to live intentional in your physical well-being?
247. How can I add value to you, each day; what actions do I do that makes you feel the most loved by me?
248. Have we settled for the status quo in life and stopped pursuing God's best?
249. Is there an area of life that seems complacent that we need to claim new territory over?
250. Have we negotiated our future for an immediate payoff?
251. Where do you see the most growth in your life?
252. How are you taking small steps toward your ideal future?
253. What small measurable step do we need to meet our financial goals?
254. What small measurable step do we need to experience greater communication?
255. What small measurable step do we need to meet our physical goals?
256. What small measurable step do we need to take to secure our family's well-being?
257. What small measurable step do we need to take to secure our connection sexually?
258. *Never* and *Always*, help to define boundaries: what are some of yours? I will …
259. What will we never compromise? How would you finish this statement: We will never …
260. What are we committed to ALWAYS do?
261. When you think about your dream and truly envision it, instead of asking how do I get there ask; how did I get here?
262. How would you finish this thought: We will always …
263. Zig Ziglar said you must plan to win; how are you planning and expecting to win in your life?
264. How can we make memories with our family this week/month, year?
265. What is our desired result for our life and marriage? What do we both agree on that we really, really want?
266. What makes you feel cherished, respected, honored, fulfilled, valued?
267. What values make you feel fulfilled or, if missing, make you feel confined or unfulfilled?
268. What values cause you to feel angst if they're taken away or lacking in your life?
269. What values do we share in common and how do they impact our decisions?
270. How can we ensure we honor our core values and keep them at the forefront of our decision making?
271. What helps you feel successful or at peace?
272. In your relationships, what characteristics do you deem most important?
273. Where do you feel vulnerable that I could pray with you about?
274. If you could live in a different era of time, which era would you choose and why?

275. What are some practical ways we can keep God first in our life and marriage?
276. What is God speaking to you or teaching you?
277. What are three things you are most grateful for in your life?
278. What was "the high" of your day? What was "the low"?
279. What are 3 attributes that most describe God to you? How do they inspire, your best?
280. What brings you joy?
281. What can you not imagine doing in life?
282. What would you do if you NEVER got paid a penny?
283. Where is the greatest evidence of the fruit/success in your life?
284. What subjects or activities do people continually seek you out for advice?
285. How can you guard your private time and our private time for God?
286. How can you get some quality time for yourself this week? Is there an activity that would be fun for you to do?
287. Describe your dream home; what does it look like?
288. How can we spend some quality time together as a family?
289. In three to five words, how do you think God describes you?
290. What do you value the most about our life?
291. How can we simplify life?
292. How can we create more margin in our life?
293. What have we obligated ourselves to out of fear?
294. What good things do we need to clear off our schedule to make room for great things?
295. What do we need to add to our schedule that replenishes us?
296. Look at the activities on your schedule this week and discern; will this activity help or hinder our desired outcome as a couple?
297. What do we want to add to our schedule that we love to do and want to do more of?
298. If you could add one thing to your schedule each day/week/month, what would you want to add?
299. What do we need to make sure doesn't get crowded out of our life?
300. What are our biggest time wasters?
301. What activities bring about the greatest reward/results that we can do together as a couple?
302. What are our NON-negotiables?
303. What will you safeguard and fight for at ALL costs?
304. What are you unwilling to sacrifice?
305. What opportunities do you need to say yes to and what opportunities move you away from pursuing your purpose?
306. What disciplines do you need to add to help you reach your goals?
307. As we look at our schedule, when is the best time for us to reflect and hold meaningful conversation?
308. Do our actions and decisions help us to move toward our desired goals as a couple?
309. How can we add value to one another and our kids, right now, in this season of life?
310. What activities are we doing that produce the greatest outcomes in every are of our life? (financially, spiritually, socially, physically, emotionally)

311. How can we parent as one, supporting one another, and make decisions together as a couple?
312. If you could change one thing about our home, what would you change?
313. How can we demonstrate unconditionally love for our kids, without condoning bad behavior, and live in unity regardless of their actions?
314. If you could change your thinking, what would you change?
315. How can we communicate and foster a healthy and safe place for one another and our kids?
316. What can we do to foster healthy friendships and improve our social connection as a couple?
317. Fill in the blank: When it comes to our financial future and my relationship with money, one thing I'd like to focus on is _____.
318. What practical steps can we take to secure our future financially?
319. What are some practical steps that I could do to help ensure our connection and physical intimacy?
320. How do you describe humility? Who do you know that best demonstrates it?
321. What are you most looking forward to in this next year?
322. Fill in the blank: I am most in the mood when _____?
323. When do you feel the most heard?
324. What does healthy communication and connection look like to you?
325. It's been said, failing to plan is planning to fail; what do we need to plan for to ensure connection and fulfillment?
326. Have we made concessions or compromises in pursuing our dreams or God's purpose?
327. What's your favorite quote?
328. If you could live into a single word this year, what would it be?
329. What's your favorite food?
330. What's the best meal you've ever had?
331. What's your favorite food dish I make for you?
332. What's your favorite recipe?
333. If you could only eat one food for the rest of your life, what would it be?
334. What nostalgic items seemed super cool to you as a kid that you think should come back?
335. What characteristic do you most appreciate in a friend?
336. How would your best friend describe you?
337. What activities help to rekindle our connection?
338. If tomorrow were declared "NATIONAL YOU" day, what would we do to celebrate?
339. How would someone you just met describe you?
340. What's the weirdest gift you ever received?
341. What's the most amazing thing that's ever happened to you?
342. How has God surprised you?
343. What's the best piece of advice you ever received?
344. What's the worst advice you ever heard?
345. It's been said any weakness is just an over-utilization of a strength; what's yours?
346. What's your favorite animal and why?
347. If you could be any animal, what would you be?

348. What consumes your thinking?
349. What do you dream about doing?
350. What do you dream about having?
351. If I could read your mind right now, what would I learn?
352. How do you feel overworked right now?
353. What lies or limitations are you believing about yourself? What's the real truth?
354. What you feed grows; what you starve dies. What thoughts are you entertaining?
355. Since success and failures are largely the results of our habits, what habits would you like to create together?
356. How can we plan for success?
357. What "stinking thinking" do you wish you could get rid of once and for all?
358. What are you most determined to have, do, or possess?
359. We are you most committed to?
360. Which do you prefer, dinner around the kitchen table or dining out? And, why?
361. How would you finish this sentence; in our family we … one another?
362. If your life we captured on a billboard, how would your tagline/motto read?
363. What has God promised you?
364. What are some Scriptural promises that you want to hold on to?
365. What limitations are we entertaining that we need to let go of as a couple?
366. How has God used the "waste years" or in between times of life to prepare you for His best?
367. What makes you feel rested, inspired or rejuvenated?
368. What habits do we need to recommit to, in order to optimize our efforts and best live our ideal marriage?
369. Are there areas of our life or character that we need to realign, in order to live our ideal marriage?
370. What's a local attraction you'd like to visit?
371. What's a new restaurant you'd like to try?
372. What limitations or impossibilities are between us and the complete joy of living our purpose in marriage?
373. Is there anywhere in life that you feel stuck in the "how loop"? (For example: How will I? How can I make this happen?)
374. What would you start right now if you had all the resources in place?
375. What's your top priority for today?
376. What's your top priority for this week?
377. What's your top priority for this year?
378. What 'input' fosters the best 'output'?
379. We find what we are looking for; here's what I love about you.
380. You inspire me when …
381. I feel the most loved by you when we are …
382. I love how you …
383. I will never forget the time …
384. My favorite memory of you is when …
385. The best gift you ever gave me was …
386. You are so good at …
387. I like it when you …

388. I feel the most connected when we …
389. You turn me on when …
390. I feel the most content when we are …
391. I love how we …
392. I love spending time with you …
393. My favorite thing about you is …
394. The thing I admire most about you is …
395. Your (insert character quality) is the thing I respect most about you
396. I trust you because you …
397. I love how you serve me when you …
398. I appreciate how you always …
399. I love you and I want you to know, I noticed how you …
400. How can we concentrate our attention on God's intention, daily?
401. In what areas do we need to most focus our attention?
402. In what areas do we need to redirect or change our attention?
403. What concerns you or steals your joy?
404. Couples who live for a greater purpose-together-thrive; what do you think our purpose is?
405. What ground rules can we put in place to safeguard healthy conversations that stimulate growth?
406. Do you like to hear compliments? Read compliments? Or Both?
407. What do we both desire? What do we really, really, really want?
408. What's most important now?
409. How can we create an environment that leads us to be successful?
410. What threats hold the potential of leading us off course or distract us from our vision?
411. How can we safeguard against those threats?
412. What daily and weekly practices do we need to establish to defend our purpose?
413. What intentional habits do we need to practice to reach our goals?
414. How can we add value to one another?
415. How can we add value to others?
416. What do you want to focus on today, and how can I best serve you?
417. What areas do we need to change to produce optimal results?
418. How do we move forward from here?
419. How can I better fight for your dreams?
420. Instead of living resigned, how can we live our design?
421. How would you finish this statement; we live to …
422. How would you finish this statement; we love to …
423. How would you finish this statement; we enjoy …
424. How would you finish this statement; we feel most useful when …
425. In a crowd we feel the most comfortable when …
426. We are passionate about …
427. We won't stop until we …
428. If we could accomplish one thing in life together, it would be …
429. How do we protect our purpose?

430. How does our common purpose allow opportunity for both of us to use our strengths to contribute to the overall dream?
431. What are our most important qualities, attributes, and beliefs as a couple?
432. When you think of legacy, what do you want to be remembered for?
433. If you died today, would you have any regrets?
434. Is there anything you regret doing that you can change to move forward?
435. When you think about the choices and decisions you need to make; what causes you to say yes and what causes you to say no? *Why* would you move forward? *Why* would you stand still? *Why* would you say no and walk away?
436. Are there any areas of life you feel like you just maintaining *the status quo* that you'd like to dream bigger for?
437. Instead of worrying about retiring, what would you love doing every day for the rest of your life?
438. How can we spend more time together enjoying life?
439. What spiritual activities do you enjoy doing?
440. What physical activities do you enjoy doing?
441. What intellectual activities do you enjoy doing?
442. What are your favorite interests?
443. What are your favorite hobbies?
444. How do you like to fill your free time?
445. What are your favorite sports, to watch?
446. What are your favorite sports, to play?
447. What do we love doing?
448. What brings us both joy?
449. What would we do if we never got paid for it?
450. What talents or gifts would you like to be using more often?

As you close out your time with your couple. Take a moment to do the following:

- ☐ Debrief Learnings and Checkpoints
- ☐ Check your Where We Want to Be Chart. Did you hit the initiative of the desired outcome? Give yourself a check mark for each accomplished task.
- ☐ Point your Couple to their next steps.
- ☐ Remind them of their learnings and schedule your follow up call.
- ☐ At the end of your day, enroll your client in the membership.
- ☐ Confirm they can get logged into the membership site.
- ☐ Help them understand how to utilize the membership community.
- ☐ Inform them of typical call times.
- ☐ Pray with them.
- ☐ Hand them their gift book from us.
- ☐ Point out additional resources for conversation starters, parenting principles, communication hacks and other items found in the back of their reboot workbook.

NOTES

NOTES

NOTES

NOTES

As you close out your time with your couple. Take a moment to do the following:

- ☐ Debrief Learnings and Checkpoints
- ☐ Check your Where We Want to Be Chart. Did you hit the initiative of the desired outcome? Give yourself a check mark for each accomplished task.
- ☐ Point your Couple to their next steps.
- ☐ Remind them of their learnings and schedule your follow up call.
- ☐ At the end of your day, enroll your client in the membership.
- ☐ Confirm they can get logged into the membership site.
- ☐ Help them understand how to utilize the membership community.
- ☐ Inform them of typical call times.
- ☐ Pray with them.
- ☐ Hand them their gift book from us.
- ☐ Point out additional resources for conversation starters, parenting principles, communication hacks and other items found in the back of their reboot workbook.

---

[i] Romans 8:28, New International Version of the Bible.
[ii] New American Standard Bible Copyright © 1960, 1962, 1963, 1968, 1971, 1972, 1973, 1975, 1977, 1995 by The Lockman Foundation, La Habra, Calif.
[iii] https://www.goodreads.com/author/quotes/1538.Stephen_R_Covey

Made in United States
Orlando, FL
02 February 2023